PENGUIN ANANDA

CAVEMAN'S SECRET SAUCE

Nimish Dayalu is the co-founder and CEO of Zoga Wellness—a hi-tech mobile application designed to help users learn and practise ancient Indian yoga and meditation. Nimish, ex-global head of people development, Moody's, is passionate about bringing a positive change in people's lives. A certified yoga teacher on a path of mind training, he has yoga in his DNA—his direct lineage is from the world-famous Iyengar yoga family.

T0006294

Caveman's SECRET SAUCE

FINDING ANSWERS TO THE WORLD'S OLDEST QUESTIONS

Nimish Dayalu

PENGUIN
ANANDA

An imprint of Penguin Random House

PENGUIN ANANDA

USA | Canada | UK | Ireland | Australia
New Zealand | India | South Africa | China

Penguin Ananda is part of the Penguin Random House group of companies
whose addresses can be found at global.penguinrandomhouse.com

Published by Penguin Random House India Pvt. Ltd
4th Floor, Capital Tower 1, MG Road,
Gurugram 122 002, Haryana, India

First published in Penguin Ananda by Penguin Random House India 2022

ISBN 9780143459163

Typeset in Sabon MT Std by MAP Systems, Bengaluru, India

www.penguin.co.in

In fond memory of my father—Air Vice-Marshal V.K. Dayalu

Contents

Author's Note

Having spent close to two decades dabbling in Indian yogic and meditative practices, I set out to make this knowledge more palatable to today's reader. It wasn't as straightforward, though. The seeds were planted much earlier.

While working my corporate job, I would often find myself wondering whether something was amiss. This inquiry would often take me close to nature, especially the Indian and Nepalese Himalayas, and give me an opportunity to ask questions and seek answers. These journeys inspired me to go back to my roots.

I come from the Iyengar yoga family and was exposed to yoga very early in life. As a lifestyle choice, it changes you from the inside out. I felt that creating a higher level of awareness could be my gateway to living in the moment and that all the strength I needed was within me. That was when I decided to dive deep into yoga and share my learning. I founded Zoga in 2021, a hi-tech mobile app to share ancient Indian yogic and meditative practices.

The challenges I have faced and the tools I have used to overcome can be used by anyone. This is how the book was conceived: there are modern problems and there are ancient solutions; the two had to be reconciled. The book is inspired by real-life events but also contains myths, folktales and lessons derived from various Indian traditions. The central idea, however, revolves mainly around Advaita philosophy and its derivative yogic teachings. These teachings are presented in an adventurous, funny and thought-provoking narrative with ancient secrets as the key ingredient in *Caveman's Secret Sauce*.

Introduction

There is something mystical about the Himalayas. It has been the preferred destination for sages and yogis alike. In Indian culture, it is considered to be the land of the gods. It exists in the perfect harmony of peace and purity, and allows one to delve deep into the labyrinths of one's own mind. It has fascinated me ever since I was a young man and I have frequently found myself in the lap of the Himalayas over the years. The experiences, to be honest, were not always pleasant.

I was once caught in a snow blizzard on a solo winter expedition to the Everest base camp; the visibility was less than 10 metres. My son was only two months old at that time. Wet and hypothermic, I almost broke down. Would my infant son grow up without his father? That was the last thought I remember. As luck would have it, I was rescued by a Sherpa who miraculously appeared from somewhere that day. My heart was and has ever since been full of gratitude.

This book is inspired by real-life events and experiences over a couple of decades with a smattering of fiction. I realized over the years that my brain was so wired and programmed that I was functioning more like a programmed robot. Was I living my life or was it someone else's? Were the decisions I was making even mine? Can I be happy? What am I doing in this world?

I set off to find answers to some of these questions. Upon exploring ancient Indian scriptures, I embarked on a path of mind-training. As I dove deeper, I spent more time practising and teaching yoga and meditation. The knowledge, along with new experiences, created a higher awareness and the realizations were profound.

This is Jeet's story: he had a job with a large corporation, a family and a seemingly happy life. He left everything to go on a journey and live in a mountain cave by himself. He had spent a fair bit of time in the wilderness by himself and was confident of surviving. Little did he know what was coming his way and how it would impact his life.

Jeet meets some interesting people along the way from varied walks of life. He also meets Adi; an immortal being living in this region for a long time. Adi unravels forgotten Indian wisdom and folklore that would help Jeet live with higher awareness. Come and join him on his awe-inspiring spiritual quest, high up in the mighty Himalayas.

Chapter 1

Chasing Butterflies

A deafening sound startles me and shakes me up. Whump!

I look up the mighty mountain and watch in open-mouthed astonishment as the avalanche rushes towards me. My whole life flashes before my eyes. Is this it? *Run*, I tell myself and take that leap. Luckily, I manage to enter the cave just in time. In a matter of seconds, it is pitch dark and an eerie silence ensues. I take a deep breath and my racing heart slowly fills up with gratitude. That was close!

The cave entrance is blocked. Sensing that the danger has been averted, I use my wooden staff to find a way out. It is pointless—the cotton-candy snow has transformed into concrete now. *But*, I tell myself, *it is just a matter of time before the sun thaws the entrance and rescues me from darkness.* The thought brings calm . . . Just like this fire, which I have been making every few hours to keep myself warm.

I cannot tell how much time has gone by—maybe some days or nights—before I could have any success in my attempt to exit the cave. This time, when I push through the frozen entrance to dislodge the blockade, it moves. It isn't as hard as concrete any more; I am drenched in sweat as I dig furiously.

One last push and . . . I am out! Ah! Thank god for light! And thank god for darkness, without which I would not have known the divinity of light. I fold my hands in a namaste and place them on my chest, bow my head and close my eyes. Some might call it a prayer—for me, it's an expression of gratitude.

I am greeted with a cool sensation on my sweaty body. The wind, coming from the snowy mountains in the north, caresses me. I turn around, thinking somebody has tapped my bare back. 'Good morning, old friend,' I wish to say to the wind. How incredible it feels to face the sheer force of nature without shielding yourself! My feet, pressed against the fresh, moist grass, feel a tingling sensation flowing through my nerves and on to my toes and soles. This single sensation leads to many more in other parts of my body, all the way up my spine. It's surreal. It's the feeling of being alive—fully alive!

The wind hastens as if it wants to carry on the conversation even more intensely. There are no words; only susurrations, and some sighing and soughing. It does not waste any time in expressions, words or phrases, and goes straight to my soul. I pay close attention to the wind, its sounds, sensations and all the things that it is trying to convey. What does it say? 'The Times . . . They Are A-Changing.' I hum the song that I feel is blowing in the wind. The coldness of winter is leaving, to the other side of the earth, until the next time. Prepare yourself for the spring, dear old friend, it says. Or that's what I hear. You may say that it is only my mind, trying to play a trick on me in the guise of the wind. But isn't it always the mind, manifesting its will on the material world? What is real and what is not? Who decides?

A butterfly catches my attention, interrupting my thoughts. It is resting on a rock, soaking up warm sunshine. The colours are vivid: red outlined by brown outlined by black outlined by red again. Then there are white dots scattered over its body. Its wings are fluttering, so I am having a hard time counting the colours.

As soon as I raise my right hand to reach out to the little beauty, the fluttering quickens and it glides off. My head turns and my gaze follows its flight. It sits on a primrose flower close by, feasting on its nectar. Still, it wouldn't settle on the flower for long; flying from here to there and back again, and repeat; which reminds me of the human mind. From this flower to the next, the butterfly visits one after the other. As if it is so busy chasing an endless series of pleasures that it fails to see its own beauty. Don't we tend to do that too?

It's only when we are out in the wild—with nothing on our schedules and nowhere to escape to—that we encounter this bizarre thing that is referred to as the self.

I turn towards the white mountains in the north, standing in all their glory since time immemorial.

In their own strange way, they do something to me every time I look at them. How do I describe this feeling that transcends the realm of the ordinary human lexicon? I don't have the answer. No word can capture the wholeness of my experience, even when I have been looking for it in the deepest corners of my mind. For now, all I can say is that when I look at these mountains, it fills me with sheer joy and a deep sense of longing, as though it's where my soul comes from and it's where it seeks to return. The sense of belongingness comes naturally in the presence of mountains. Mountains! Yes. So grand and mighty they are! Standing tall, witnessing generations of human beings along with their cultures and beliefs come and go, while they stay. They look pristine and yet cold, sometimes to the point of being harsh. Thankfully, their beauty or coldness doesn't discriminate, unlike the powerful of the other world, where I come from. Mountains are mighty and noble, not mighty and mean. They inspire you, make you feel humble, not small, even when they are easily capable of doing that. This is what makes them . . . sublime? *Sublime*, I whisper to myself. *Ah! That's the word I have been looking for.* The answers, sometimes, are flowing all around us, as much trying to find us as we are trying to find them. I feel complete. A feeling that I have missed in the corridors of my office where I spent countless hours of my life. Maybe life existed there as well; it's just that I could not find time or space to appreciate it inside those tinted-glass walls.

I think of the butterfly again, which is not to be seen any more. *Where has it gone?* I ask myself and the surroundings. There is silence, as if they are hiding the butterfly in a game of hide-and-seek. But, where is it? Vanished completely, no trace left of it anywhere. I scrutinize every flower in the vicinity. Spring has just arrived, so they are in plenty, blooming in their early youth. With as many colours—if not more—as I traced on the wings of the butterfly. Then, after a long, careful look, I finally see it, sitting on the first flower once again. I smile to myself and take a deep breath. I can feel the brightness, the warmth of the sun, along with the cool wind on my back, bringing the freshness of melting snow. I feel a sense of belongingness to all these things. I spread my arms wide apart and feel the vastness of all the life that I sense around. 'I feel alive,' I whisper it; not once, not twice, but multiple times.

'Excuse me?' a voice interrupts me. 'Excuse me? How's it going?' it says.

I open my eyes. There is a lanky young man, with a rucksack on his back and hands on his hips, standing in front of me. He is staring at me as if he has discovered some mythical creature in the Himalayas. I look at him in silence for a few moments as I lower my arms and take a step forward. He appears a little tired, his hair waving in all directions.

'Why are you looking at me like that?' he asks. 'It reminds me of my college professors. And that is not a happy thought, believe me.' He strokes his hair and chuckles. 'What were you doing there? I am just curious.'

I still don't say a word and keep looking at him keenly. 'Ah, the youth!' says my mind, 'not very different from butterflies.'

'Come on, I was joking.' There is a pause, but not for long. 'I don't think I am going to get any answers from you,' he says, while shaking his head. 'At least, tell me this, sir. What were you doing?'

This time I feel obligated to respond. 'Nothing,' I say, with a sheepish smile.

'Nothing?' his eyes widen. Clearly my response hasn't satisfied all the curiosity that resides in him. 'What do you mean, nothing? Look at this,' he imitates my earlier posture, smiling and stretching his arms far and wide. 'This has to mean something.'

'Does it have to?'

'I don't know what that means. I don't know why anybody would want to do nothing. Oh god, please help me,' he folds his hands and laughs. 'I mean, I get it if you don't want to answer. But hey, come on.'

'You know what? Actually, you are right. I wasn't doing nothing.'

'Thank god,' he sighs, looking up. 'I mean, if you asked me this question, I would also hesitate a little but would surely answer. I would say, I am hiking. In fact, I would introduce myself and say, "Hello, I am Dev." And in general, if you ask me about what I do, then I would say I have just got into a college where I am studying . . . okay, I don't do much studying; still, that counts. But at least we all are doing something here in this world, aren't we? So tell me, dear old man, what are you doing here?'

'I am living and hello to you, Dev. I am Jeet.'

He shrugs and examines me from head to toe. His doubts are visible even to the naked eye.

'Living? We all are living here. You are living, I am living. Those people in my college, they are living. Those sheep over there, they are living too. Aren't we all living?'

'I don't know, are we?'

'Why not? We are definitely not dead. What is not dead has to be alive, isn't it? So, they must be living.' Then he mumbles briefly, 'Don't confuse me now.'

We look at each other and laugh. When you meet someone at an office, studio, supermarket, party or anywhere in the world of social contracts, you meet them as somebody, the role that you are playing. The conversations there are restricted in many ways. But here, in the wild, we are talking as a man would talk to a man. Without any pretence, without any protocols— it's liberating! 'Anyway, that was not my question,' he says. 'My question was more about, umm, what you do. To put it more simply, who are you?'

'Why do we have to tie our identities with the labour that we do?' I decide to put an end to my questions and explain the point this time. 'We are something and then there is something we do. I was in hospitality at one point, then I worked with a large financial institution . . .'

'That would have been my first guess.'

'Ha ha,' I continue. 'And then a yoga teacher. Does that make me three people? No, right? Our jobs are part of what we do, not the entirety of our existence. It would be a sad world if it worked like that, wouldn't it?'

He thinks about it for a while and then he smiles. 'You are something else,' he says. 'I have never heard this sort of thing.'

'That must be a compliment, I believe.'

He laughs and I join him as we start to walk together. The connection between two human beings becomes apparent when their expressions synchronize and their bodies align along with their minds. 'I am not going to argue with you on this,' he says, as we share another laugh together.

'Here,' I say, 'have some berries. I picked them in the morning. You will like them. A little bit of sweetness is not bad.'

'No, not at all. Thank you for these.' He puts one in his mouth. 'Really good,' he says. 'Ah! It's sweet and a little bit sour too. Nice, nice . . . but, is that all you eat?'

'Ha ha,' I laugh heartily. 'You're something too, man. Well, it depends . . . depends on what I find here to eat. But yes, berries, they never cease to amaze.'

'Are you *really* living here? Wait . . . no, I didn't mean the existence thing,' he laughs. 'I mean, living-living. That is, have you found a place here to stay?'

'Yes.'

'Really? That is so cool. When did you come here?'

'I came here during the first snow of last winter. Last year, I mean. So . . . it's been a few months.'

'So, where is your bungalow? Have you found one in the mountains or is it somewhere far?'

'Umm—' I was going to answer but he goes on.

'Either way, I am impressed. I am telling you that.'

'Sorry to disappoint you, but it's neither.'

'Damn, no?'

'Don't worry. You might like this. See that place over there,' I point towards the cave. 'That has been my humble abode for some time.'

'In that waterfall?'

'No. Right there, in the cave.'

The waterfall is right beside the cave. I hear its burbling all day long as the water pours down and streams through the grassland. It's serene to look at, especially in the morning when the sunrays spread into the colours of a rainbow.

'I don't know what to say about that, but I am so tired that I wouldn't mind resting in a cave.'

'Come on, then.'

We walk together with the sun behind us. I enter the cave and Dev follows me.

'Fascinating,' he says. 'It's almost better than a house.'

'Isn't this,' I say, laughingly, 'an exotic piece of architecture?'

He nods and scrutinizes every corner of the cave. It is dark but not completely, so he could see some parts of it. There are faces and figurines carved on the rocks; some human, some mythical. Dev looks and sniffs at the rocks as I had done when I first came here. More than seeing or sniffing, I suppose, he too feels the energy of it. People, for millennia, have meditated in these places and whether or not you find any evidence of that, these places still speak of what they have witnessed in the past. It happens everywhere, if you notice. Not only do places leave their memories on people, but the opposite is also true.

'It is surprisingly warm here,' Dev says. The silence of the place is suddenly shaken. His voice reverberates in the interiors of the cave. 'Where is your stuff?' he asks.

'What stuff? There is no stuff. There is just one thing and that thing is me,' I say softly. 'Isn't that enough?'

'I am—somewhat—getting your strange philosophies now. Hey, tell me, is this one of those man-made caves?'

'No, it's more of a natural one. As you can see from the shape of the entrance, uneven ground and . . . see these rocks? They were carved by nature for millions of years. Not the drawings, of course.'

'Yes.'

'That's nature at work for you. The Himalayas were formed when the Indian plate and the Eurasian plate collided. Some of the caves in this area are millions of years old.'

'That is even older than you,' he laughs.

'Ha ha,' I join him. 'Slightly. But yes, they are even older than humanity.'

'Hmm . . . By the way,' he speaks after some time, 'do you have some water by any chance? I hope you do, because my throat is really parched.'

I offer him water immediately. I had brought it from the stream earlier this morning.

'Oh my . . . it's freezing cold, this water. Tastes really good, though, I have to say. I don't know if it's my tiredness or the water. Or have you put something in it?'

'I have not. And does it really matter whether it is the tiredness or the water?'

'No, I guess not. Hey, have you lived all your life in caves and stuff?' he asks. 'I mean, looking at your tattoos and all, it sounds like a dumb question, but you know what I mean, right?'

'I think I understand.' There is a smile on my face. 'I have lived what you would describe a normal life.'

'Tell me about it,' he says. 'No . . . wait. Tell me later. I think I am going to sleep. Been hiking for twelve hours straight. Can't stay awake for a minute now. Hope you don't mind.'

'Not at all. Please go ahead. I am sorry I don't have a bed for you.'

'No problem, I have one.' He takes out his sleeping bag and spreads it on the ground. I look at the faces on the rocks. Thinking of the people who would have lived here, I close my eyes for the next few minutes.

'Good night,' I say to Dev, but he is snoring.

Dev sleeps through the evening and into the night. It's good to have company sometimes; it's been days. I was hoping that Adi would show up, but that does not seem likely now. Strange are his ways. Quietly he goes and mysteriously he reappears. I wonder where he is and what he is doing tonight. Soon, I fall asleep too.

There comes the morning, and I walk towards the entrance of the cave. The sun has not come out yet, but I can see it is on its way behind the mountain. The breeze is gentle; it sprinkles refreshing mist on my face. I sit down and close my eyes.

As I open my eyes, I can see the sun breaking through clouds. It sets the day into motion: the sky turns brighter and birds replace the stars on its canvas. I cross the stream and walk uphill, into the forest. Something must be waiting, I hope. Yesterday I had set a few traps by digging some holes in the forest. The idea was to catch a rabbit. I had placed a small rock, exactly the size of the opening, right beside the hole. One end of the rock was on the ground, the other supported by a stick, which was further supported by another stick along the ground and a series of twigs placed on top of the hole. The bait (berries and rabbit-droppings) was inside the hole as well as on the surface. Any movement around the trap and the rock would fall, thereby capturing the intruder.

That was last evening. The night must have decided a rabbit's fate.

I tiptoe towards the spot. The rock is not standing any more. Good news? *It should be inside then*, I tell myself and move quickly. As I approach, I see the long, black ear pressed under the rock. There are no signs of a struggle. I lift the rock with one hand and grab the rabbit by the ear. It is unconscious; otherwise, it would have given me a hard time. I am happy to have trapped the rabbit, but somewhere deep within, I regret it too. Our mind may not be a natural habitat for conflicts, but they somehow find a way in. Folding my hands and looking up, I start to pray. 'Thank you, Mother Nature, for providing us with this wonderful gift. May the rabbit's body nourish our bodies and may its memory nourish our souls!'

When Dev wakes up, he does not waste any time and straightaway jumps on the food that I have prepared. It's soft, tender and juicy. Dev is quiet; he seems much calmer this morning. He hasn't talked much after waking up and is merely observing the food he is consuming. He is absorbing more than he is expressing. It is happening on its own; no one has done anything. You don't have to teach these things in the wild. Awareness comes naturally here.

'You seem like a good man,' he breaks his silence. 'Somebody who would get along nicely with people.'

I wait for him to continue.

'Then why are you here, living like a recluse? Shouldn't you be out there in the world? I say this only because we need more people like you. People that are kind and gentle and understanding. Don't you think that you are squandering some great opportunities by fiddling around here in the Himalayas?'

'I am living here. It is said in our ancient scriptures that one should not be led by others; instead, one should awaken his own mind, amass his own experiences and decide for himself his own path. That is precisely what I am doing.'

'I see that. But do you really need an escape?'

'This is not an escape.'

He smiles. 'Is this really important?'

'For me, being comes first. If we can live fully, experience the vastness of our life as well as that in the universe, then everything else comes after. If we don't follow this path, we might end up doing more harm than good.'

'But a lot of people are doing what they are without thinking, isn't it? Like, once I heard a wise man say— we are what we do, so we must focus on doing our jobs really well.'

'I cannot speak for others, but I don't want to live a programmed life . . . doing things out of fear or anxiety. I want to give the life within me a chance to express itself.'

'And what does that mean? I mean, how do you just live?'

'Just look around. See those flowers. See that bird. Why do you think they exist? Do they need to have any passion? Are they made for bouquets and cages?'

'No.'

'Then why are they there?'

'They are just there, I guess. To exist. To grow and flourish.'

'And so are you and I, my dear.'

'I see, but tell me honestly, do you think this is enough? To just live and not chase other things?'

'Well, if you see the life within you carefully, you will find a whole world inside.'

'How is that so?'

'Think about it. Every little cell in your body would not exist if it was not for the sun, the water, the earth, the air. You are not just constantly in touch with the universe, but you hold the whole universe within you.'

'I see what you mean. So, how does that shape the other things we do? I mean, what you are saying, it makes perfect sense, but how do we do our jobs in that case? Let me be straightforward here. I want to ask, what should I do? I feel really confused about my life prospects.'

'You do things which are meaningful to you and are best aligned with your life. You do it with love. You do it with care. That means you add value to your own life, as well as to the world outside. More importantly, you experience this life to the fullest as it should be.'

'I somehow keep fearing about failure. What if others go past me and I fail?'

'Well, that only happens when you think of them as others. There are no others. You help yourself by helping them and vice versa. As long as you create boundaries, suffering is inevitable.'

'It's scary too.'

'I agree. Making a big change can be very scary. But, you know what's even scarier? Living a life with regrets.'

'I get really confused. What do I do? Everyone talks about finding your passion. I don't know what that means. I don't know how to find that. How does one find meaning? Could you help me find that?'

'For that, you will have to do something for me . . . will you?'

'Yes.'

'Then here's a small task for you. Actually, two tasks. First: go and find the most beautiful butterfly in the valley.'

'Okay,' he says and runs away as soon as I finish the sentence. He slows his pace near the flowers, taking a look at each one of them and examining every butterfly that he sees. After some time, he comes back, huffing and puffing.

'Did you find it?'

'I think so. But I am confused between the one with translucent wings and the one with a sunset on it.'

'How do you feel?'

'Tired.'

'Now, go to the first butterfly you find and just follow it. Observe it. Spend time with it. Learn as many things about it as possible.'

He takes a look around and spots one sitting on a flower. He moves towards it, following every little movement. Within seconds, he gets engrossed in the details of the butterfly's colourful patterns, its structure and movements.

'How do you feel now?' I ask him once he is back.

'I feel relaxed. But I don't know how I missed this one. This has to be the most beautiful.'

I smile at him. 'That's what happens when you do any task with focus, without worrying about rewards. You don't have to go anywhere to find your passion. Simply start with the task at hand and do it with great care.'

'And where do I begin? I hope I am not asking too many questions.'

'Begin by living,' I say, 'and no, you are asking good questions. It's incredible that people don't ask more questions. Most of them go about their lives without much introspection to understand their purpose.'

'Life is short, as they say.'

'Is it, though? The 27 club in the music world has some illustrious names, names of legends that left us when they were only twenty-seven years old: Jimi Hendrix, Kurt Cobain, Jim Morrison and many more. "Only twenty-seven years old!" most would say. If life is lived well and we are wise about the time that we have, then life is long enough. It's not the length of your life that matters but the depth. Every moment holds infinite value, and if you learn the art of living it fully, you would feel that you have lived indefinitely. So, go my friend . . . and LIVE.'

'You are right. I guess, it's time to start living,' he says and hugs me. It was unexpected, but emotional. He does not utter a word for the next few minutes and neither do I. We simply sit next to each other and observe the mountains in silence. 'I will take a walk,' he says and gets up.

An hour or so later, Dev says goodbye. He has to go back today.

'I am so happy that we met,' he says.

'So am I. Take care of yourself, and don't miss the butterfly.'

He smiles as we shake hands.

The next minute, I see him walking towards the village where he came from. There's a butterfly flying above his head; the two seem to be moving together. It's a sign! I know he has a lot of questions still lingering in his mind. There is confusion too. But I sense that he is much more at peace with himself. The butterfly will guide him.

I am back in the cave now. Something inside me tells me that Adi will visit tonight. Now I am just sitting and waiting and hoping that my instincts have told me the truth. Wait . . . I can hear footsteps slowing down outside the cave . . . could it be him? And now, there is his voice. Finally, he has arrived.

Chapter 2

Bird in a Golden Cage

It's a blissful sight! Adi is sitting by the fire. I look at the embers glowing at the end of his pipe; a ring of smoke surfaces and rises until it stretches outwards, unfolds and slowly disappears. The reddish tinge of fire has spread in the cave, with a layer of darkness surrounding it.

His face reflects the redness as he takes another puff. He has brought—as he does every time—the finest of herbs that one can find in these divine mountains: some for fragrance, some for the torch and some for the smoke. He knows these mountains well. No! He knows them all too well. I look at him, still in awe, still wondering what brings him here each time.

It seems like yesterday when he first showed up at the cave. There was a sound as I sat in the dark. First it was the air that blew, then it turned into a whistle, and then . . . was someone playing a flute? I could not believe my ears, but as the sound went on, I could no longer hold on to my disbelief. Quietly, I peeked through the entrance.

'Is there a leopard inside?' his deep voice echoed through the cave.

It was dark and I could not see exactly who stood there. Surely it was a human voice—that much I knew. So, I stepped forward and walked towards the entrance; a myriad of thoughts flooded my mind. Hosting a guest in my apartment was one thing, but here . . . and who was the guest?

It was a full-moon night, and I could see him standing, with the moon shining—and hiding—partially behind his long hair. He was carrying a staff in one hand and a flute in the other. Behind him, the waterfall shimmered in the moonlight.

'No leopards, right?' he asked, taking a glimpse inside.

'If there was a leopard, I wouldn't be here—'

'That's good,' he did not let me finish and walked in. My gaze followed his footsteps in amazement. He continued, 'I always check if there is a leopard inside.' He kept his staff near the corner as we stood facing each other. He was tall and broad, and spoke in a deep voice. 'Once I entered a cave and you know what I found inside? I found leopard cubs. Really small, maybe a few days old. I was so intrigued by those little bundles of joy that I started playing with them. Then I realized that their mother was standing behind me.

I turned around and there she was. She stared at me and I stared at her. I did not fear her for I knew she would smell my fear and rip my flesh off. The staring went on. It turned out that she was kind. She waited for me to leave. I obliged, stepping backward. You should not mess with the creatures of the wild.'

I nodded. 'Would you like some, umm . . . ' I wanted to extend my hospitality, but as I was saying this, I realized that there was nothing to offer. I swallowed my words immediately.

'Have you had your food?' he asked me gently, placing his hand on my shoulder.

'Yes, I have,' I said, still unsure about the identity of this man.

'Very well, I have had it too,' he said, as if he could read my thoughts.

'That's good,' I said, wondering what I could have offered if he had been hungry.

Here I was, eyeing this mysterious man who had just shown up out of nowhere and was casually speaking of leopards one minute and inquiring about my diet, the other. No greetings, no introductions, nothing. It felt odd. Why was he the way he was? As I would soon discover, he did not know (or perhaps had forgotten) the customs of society. In a really strange way, the big fellow was a child.

As I lit the fire and saw his face for the first time, I was taken back. He seemed like a man from a different world. Long hair, enviously well built. His hair was matted, forehead smeared with ash. His face was covered in a thick, dense beard. When he smiled, his eyes, not his lips hidden behind the dense beard, gave that indication. His aura was something else— something that I hadn't experienced before. I have never understood any definition of beauty, but in that moment, I got my answer: you find something beautiful when you see its spirit breaking all the barriers and speaking to you. That's exactly what his presence did.

He laid his flute on the ground and continued talking. I was even more surprised that he was speaking to me in a language I knew.

'I have spent some time in this cave. It is beautiful,' he said, as he sat down and looked around. I followed and sat next to him. 'What a place to be in!'

'I am sorry, I did not know you were here—'

'It's all right,' he said and smiled.

Perhaps he did not understand what I was trying to say; perhaps he did understand without me saying it. But in that moment, I felt a little awkward, as though I had made a mistake by staying here. I was trying to say that it was wrong on my part to seize his property and I could leave if he wished to.

'I am sorry I occupied your place,' I said, to make my point clear.

He laughed, loud and for long. And when he laughed, the sound echoed in the cave. 'My place?' He laughed again. 'What is my place or your place? It is just a place.'

Clearly, he did not understand the concept of private property—and John Locke, after having fought for this idea centuries ago, wouldn't be too pleased, I thought and smiled.

'Let me tell you a story,' he said. 'Would you like to hear one?'

'Sure, why not?' I said. As a child, I used to hear stories about mysterious men and caves in the mountains. Now, it felt as though I was becoming a part of it.

He searched for a piece of cloth that he was carrying and took out a pipe. Then he put some herbs in it and lit it. I looked at him intently. He picked up his flute and started playing. I was confused. Where was the story he promised? After he finished playing the piece, he kept the flute aside and began:

Let me tell you a story. A story of a man. A story of people. Of the questions they relentlessly ask and the answers I tirelessly repeat.

Where is your house? they ask. Where is it?

Why do I need a house? I reply. Why does anybody need one?

You need a house to cover yourself from the heat of the summer. Don't you understand this simple fact of life?

The cool shade of a big tree is enough for me. I understand that much.

What about the winters when it gets cold and the tree cannot offer you warmth?

There is fire in the forest and in funeral pyres. The dead can very much save a life while saying goodbye to the world.

Isn't that strange? Aren't you weird?

What is weird? What is strange? That I don't discriminate? That I see fire as fire and not something else? Only if you discriminate would you find it strange. Society discriminates. I don't. For me the fire offers warmth, to man and animal, to rich and poor alike. That is all.

And what do you do in rains? You cannot sit next to the fire then, can you?

I walk into the mountains, where there are no clouds. The more it rains, the higher I climb. Beyond the clouds I go and touch the sky where it rains, not frost and water, but blessings and joy.

Who are you?

Are you some god?

How can you go to the heavens?

Have you asked yourself this question: Who are you? Forget the heavens and gods, forget the world and what lies beyond it, just look closer and ask yourself: Who am I? Now, let me answer your question. Who am I? I am the caged bird in you that longs to get out. I am in me, I am in you, I am everywhere. I am the bird that you don't let out. I am that bird. The bird that reminds you every day of freedom, but you ignore me.

He stood up now and sang the last part.

I am the bird you ignore. I am the bird, I am the bird.

He sang and spread his arms like wings and twirled in bliss.

There was wisdom in everything he said or did. Words were a part of it, only a small part, though. Language, I realized in that moment, could be valuable in certain matters and limiting in others. The way he moved, it made me see depth in the simplest of things. How easy it was to experience the joy of life in his company!

'Just relax,' he paused to say and continued twirling. I stared at him with my eyes wide open as he stepped back and disappeared. *Could it have been a dream?* I thought to myself in the morning, but the trail of his big feet in the snow confirmed that it hadn't . . . and so did his subsequent visits.

That was three months ago. Tonight, I feel no different either. I still wonder about his whereabouts, what he does when he is away, and much more.

'How come you are so different from everybody else?' I ask him. 'It is as if you are not a human but a constant stream of energy.'

He looks at me intensely and says, 'Because I am not a human,' and laughs.

I laugh too. His actions are infectious—could it be the reason why he is quarantining in the mountains? The thought makes me laugh, or maybe it's his infectious laughter. When I see him laugh, I begin to laugh. The same happens when he dances.

'If I tell you my secret, would that help?' he says, after a momentary silence.

'Why not? But only if you are fine with sharing your secret.'

'There is a thing called experience,' he takes a long pull on his pipe. 'Direct experience. That is my secret. You should seek that. Do not pay too much heed to anyone else's experience. Not even mine. What people tell you, what they believe, it is either their own experience or they are parroting someone else's. So, where is your experience? Leave everything aside and teach yourself. Find your own way. Experience yourself. What is right, what is wrong—all these questions are not meant for intellectual cajolery but to be answered within you.'

'How?' I ask with the curiosity of a child.

'Open yourself to the limitless possibilities of life. Get out of your head. Don't think. Just dance.'

'Dance? What do you mean?'

'This,' he says, as he gets up. He smiles and then he begins to move. A hand goes here and a foot goes there. He forms a mudra. The next moment, he shifts to another. First, then second; first and third; first and fourth; it goes on. He is moving from one mudra to another; rhythm is his guide. The flute is still lying on the ground, and yet, I hear its music.

The music in my head grows more intense with his movements. I can feel the ground trembling, the rocks shivering. The air seems murky all of a sudden. It is as if every cell in my body is dancing to the music. *Is this what you call direct experience*? I ask myself. But why am I still thinking?

I do not remember when he left and when I slept, and now that the morning has arrived, I lie here, watching the sunrays making their way in. I get up, and suddenly feel this yearning in me to seek this 'direct experience' with nature. I saw somewhat similar dreams too; in one of them, I was flying from one tree to another, chirping here and there, and asking, 'WHERE IS THIS EXPERIENCE?'

I walk outside, looking across the valley. The contours go up and down as far as the eye can see. I trace the contours of my own hands and feet. Isn't it the boundaries that give everything its identity? Without them, you wouldn't be you and I wouldn't be I.

After taking a bath in the waterfall, I pick some berries and start walking uphill.

Why? What am I seeking? I don't know. What I do know is that I don't know, and it is what I don't know that will take me to the world of endless possibilities. Something inside tells me that I should follow this calling. I realize now that it is important to seek than to not seek at all, and so I set out to seek.

There are flowers on either side of the path: lilies, orchids, wild roses, rhododendrons and many more that I am seeing for the first time. I raise my hand and touch these flowers, dangling in all directions. Away from this gathering, there's a snow lotus. A solitary flower with a radiant white hue. 'What a beautiful thing you are!' I say to the flower as I stop to catch my breath. I spend some time appreciating its beauty, looking at it, touching it softly. Then I move on.

Sometimes, you don't know what you are looking for until you find it; and so is the case here. I realize now how much my soul needed this tonic of wilderness. My body, already acquainted with its pace, is moving swiftly along the tides of the mountain. The poetry of nature is always alive, set in motion by the life that sprouts all around. On the one hand, I am trying to catch my breath, and on the other, I can't stop myself from singing that perfect song—'What a Wonderful World'!

Once in the forest, I see a vast spread of plants and trees, and shrubs and vines—ever-growing shades of green everywhere. There is life all around. The forest floor is soft and moist, covered in moss, fallen leaves and pine needles. Birds are singing, animals scampering and insects welcoming me with acrobatic dives. They all (except the insects) seem a little wary of my presence, but the routine goes on. One chases the other and then gets chased itself. Nature has its own way of restoring balance. Wherever I turn, I sense freshness around. Life exists in its most untouched form here. I sit in the middle of it, studying everything and marvelling, what a wonderful sight this is! The air is cool and comfortable, and there is a gentle breeze blowing.

The trees sway, rejoicing in this beautiful moment. I spend the day in nothingness and that's where I experience everything. The time simply goes by; maybe it never existed in the first place.

The sunrays never truly permeated here, and now it's beginning to turn dark; the dusk follows. There is no hurry, and so I feel no compulsion to move as I watch the darkness slowly engulfing the forest. I know I am going to spend the night in the wild. There are no caves here, nor do I look for one. It's cold, but I am not too concerned about it. I want to expose myself to all the elements and possibilities, to everything that Mother Nature has to offer. When the night arrives, I climb a tree and lie down on one of its branches. The branch is broad, not too high from the ground.

The sight of nature is mesmerizing. I am reminded of this when I turn to the sky. It is like a canopy with infinite holes in it. Stars, so many of them, twinkling. Then there are planets, three of them, not twinkling at all. What was that, a shooting star? Then comes another. One more. Many more. Should I make a wish? Umm . . . what wish? This has been my wish all along. I wanted to be here and here I am. I continue looking at the sky as the meteor shower grows intense. Now, I am reminded of my home where I would long to see this but could not. These were not the stars that one would see in a city.

The forest is glowing; green and white lights everywhere; some still, some winged. Nature's orchestra is putting on a show . . . what a time to be alive! There are so many things I would have wanted to achieve, and yet, there is nothing more rewarding than this feeling of being alive . . . truly alive. Every inch of my body responds to the beauty around; such is the power of nature.

My head is under its spell, and my toes . . . there is a tickling sensation in my feet. What is it? I raise my head, trying to see what is there. An owl has slowly hopped on to my foot. *Hoot! Hoot!* it says. It hops on to my chest, and looks at me in wonder as I am looking at it. Are we really different? I don't know. Right now, in the middle of the forest, away from any member of my species, I feel a genuine connection with this creature. It feels as if the owl is a part of me and I am a part of the owl. That we are not separate; we both are a part of nature. I wonder, what is really inside the body of the owl that is looking at me and what is really inside my body that is looking at the owl? Are these two the same or different? I think about it and fall asleep. There are no dreams tonight. Only deep sleep.

The morning arrives. Thankfully, I had a good night's sleep. Wait a second! How do we know when we have had good sleep? We never truly experience it with our conscious mind. Yet, somehow, we always know whether it was good or bad once it is over. Does that mean we are experiencing it? Who is there to experience this, if we are not awake? Was it the owl that was looking at me, observing me while I was asleep? Somehow, the thought reminds me of Adi. I wonder where he is and what he is up to this morning.

I turn to the snow-capped mountain where I wish to go. It's a beautiful day! The sun is up, illuminating the clear blue sky and making me want to go higher . . . and so, I walk.

The path is hardly visible below the dense cover of the shrubs. Perhaps people don't come to this side of the mountain often. Oh! That is why . . . there are quite a few mushrooms. Which type are they? I pick one up, sniff and eat a piece of it. It tastes a little sour, different than I would have expected. It is edible though, I can sense that. Now, I eat the rest of it as well.

A few minutes later, I feel a little dizzy. Am I tired? Am I intoxicated? What is happening? I feel my body is dissolving in the air, and I am breaking out of it. The next moment, I become a part of the air and look back at it. I see myself lying there, unconscious. *Which one is me?* I wonder.

It's not that there is no space around me. It is still there, very much there, but now, all of a sudden, it has ceased to matter . . . and so it is with time. All I see is the intensity of the universe around me, not its measurements or a sense of moments slipping by. It's all here and it's all now. I find myself on the brink of panic. My mind, accustomed to a very different world, is incapable of comprehending the vastness of this experience. I want to run away, but I am always here; I want this to get over, but I am stuck in the present moment.

What is reality? Is this real? Or was that the real me? Adi told me to experience this for myself, but I am struggling with so-called reality here. What should I do? I think for a while and then give up. Unable to find an answer, I turn and head back to where I came from. The question is, where did I come from? I have no memory of it. Struggling with all the questions, my mind gets distracted the moment it hears the sound of the flute. I cannot believe this. Is he really here?

'What are you doing?' I ask, as I see him sitting on a rock. 'Am I hallucinating or are you actually here?'

'That is not important. What is important is, how are you feeling?'

'I feel confused. What is real? Is this real or was that real?'

'Neither is real. Reality lies beyond the physical experience.'

'How do I know? How do you know? How can we know any of this, if we are restricted by our senses?'

'What is experienced through our senses is not reality. What we call reality is the illusion that has been obscured to us with the lens of our senses. You must strive to discover reality for yourself.'

'Who am I, then?'

'You will tell me who you are. Are you the body?'

'No.'

'Are you the mind?'

'No.'

'Are you your job?'

'No.'

'Are you your family or the society you live in?'

'No.'

'Are you the trillions of atoms that make you?'

'No.'

'Are you all the things that you think of yourself?'

'No.'

'Are you the voice that constantly speaks in your head?'

'No.'

'Yes, you are right. You are not this. And you are not that either. You are none of these things. You are beyond the experience of wakefulness, you are beyond the realm of this world. You are pure consciousness. Everything is changing as we speak. Your atoms are changing. Your body is changing. Your mind, your thoughts, that voice in your head—they all are changing too. What remains after this, what is beyond the wakeful experience and dream sleep, that is the real you.'

I try to think about it for a while and then release all my thoughts out into the open. The thoughts float in the air and travel, eventually leaving for the great expanse of the universe. I look at Adi and he seems to fade in this vast expanse too. Is this an illusion? I cannot tell any more what is real and what is not. So, I sit on the rock with my eyes closed and look within. I ask myself, *What is reality?* and suddenly feel all my senses going numb. Am I awake? I cannot feel, hear, see anything. The best way to describe my state is that I am alive.

Slowly, I start feeling as if no boundaries exist between the outside world and me. The illusion is that there are boundaries. The identity is illusion, not I. I am becoming the world. The feeling is beautiful. A million things are happening in my body, mind and soul. Is this the ultimate reality? Pure consciousness. Nothing else. Everything else comes and goes. It transforms into something else. But this is eternal. I don't claim

to have understood it, but I can certainly say that
I have experienced this. I have known this. I know this.
As if the bird has escaped the cage and taken its first
flight . . . and now that it has, would it like to come
back?

Chapter 3

Wind in My Sails

There are two worlds. The real world—the one we live in, explore, study, understand, where we go about our business and eventually die. The other is unreal, where we return to. Not much do we know about the latter, apart from the testimonies of a few enlightened souls. Some people believe them and some don't. The two worlds seem entirely different, often unrelated. However, if you pay close attention, there is a connection; and we hold that connection within ourselves. These two worlds, real and unreal, are joined loosely by an invisible thread: the thread of our breath. Upon realizing the value of this idea, I picked up this thread, and untangled and wove it to form the pillar of my being.

What is the nature of my existence? How do I make sense of it all with my senses limiting me? I kept asking myself these questions. It was the mind's attempt to make sense of itself, but who was in charge of the mind?

I have not left the forest since that day. The day when all the physical boundaries ceased to exist and a boundless existence seemed to take over. It was only a glimpse; a glimpse into the possibilities of what could exist beyond what we call the real. Now that I have witnessed it, I know in my heart that the unreal, in some way, is real. It exists outside our unexamined existence, but it exists. It was not a matter of belief, rather, that of experience. So, irrespective of what I believed, and what I did not, I could not deny the experience that I had. At the same time, there was a growing feeling inside me to explore these possibilities.

It all started with the breath.

The moment the heady effect of the mushroom wore off, I took a mindful, deep breath. I inhaled and exhaled and realized how this passage of air creates the bridge between life and afterlife. I followed its path inside my body as it travelled from my nose, through my windpipe and into my lungs. How magical it is! It goes in, transforms and comes out, only to repeat the same process in some other life form. In the meantime, it transforms our bodies and minds too. Breath is not a thing, it's a process, constantly changing, ceaselessly flowing from one life form to another. Very much like our life force . . . We are changing, transforming, taking rebirths every moment. Being is all there is, all there could be. It is everywhere, always present. Be, and it is—that's what I thought in that moment.

Days have come and gone by. I haven't counted how many. Solitude, in some ways, is like living outside the fabric of space and time. I know where I am and that is all that matters.

It has become slightly warm in the last few days, as the sun seems to spend a lot more time gazing at us. The patches of snow are gone. The sunlight, filtered through trees and making a moving, dappled pattern before me, permeates the air and chases darkness until dusk. The days are familiar, and yet they feel different each time. I, too, have become a familiar face in the forest. My presence no longer seems foreign to other creatures as I see them jumping around, happy and carefree. They may have accepted me as a member of the wild. Some of them come to me and pretend to talk, perhaps sharing their stories or inquiring about mine. I respond to everyone. I think it's a mistake to believe that animals don't talk; they do and they do a lot. Even plants can't resist the temptation to express their concern as they sway one way or the other. Trees go a step ahead—they play celestial symphonies by waving their branches, sharing the news of joy, sorrow and sometimes, caution. Stories in the wild are aplenty, you just need to lend a ear.

It was another beautiful day. I was sitting under the shade of a tree with my eyes closed. Birds were chirping. Leaves were rustling in the breeze. I could feel it on my face and in my hair waving behind.

And there it was . . . that sound.

I opened my eyes as I heard the music. It was Adi. I saw him standing there, playing the flute with his eyes closed. *What is he doing here?* I wondered. There were so many things I wanted to share, but the sound of his flute had me under its spell. The words would not come out, only breath remained. Even the birds had gone mysteriously quiet, and so had the rustling of leaves. There was only one sound that prevailed. The sound of the flute. It reminded me of what my father would often say, 'Don't underestimate the healing power of three things—music, stars and the forest.' I felt so blessed in that moment, it felt like my heart was about to explode with love and gratitude.

Soon, I started following the music, like the mice enchanted by the pied piper. Adi played his flute while I heaved and swayed my head. It was as if it was music, not breath, that I was inhaling and exhaling. As if I was becoming music. What was the sound, the rhythm that he was playing and I was following? The thoughts fiddled with my mind and prompted me to open my eyes. Now ... he was no longer there. One moment he appears, and the next, he disappears. I found myself breathing heavily, following the rhythm I had just absorbed. It was the same music. Ah! It was the melody of the breath that he had played. It was a beautiful sound once I started noticing it. Why did I not hear this earlier? It's the music of life, and yet, we ignore it, or in many cases, choose to remain deaf, not from our ears but from our souls.

I learnt something profound that day about breath. That it's the easiest thing to meditate upon. Who would have thought?

Breath is the key to unravelling the pre-existing happiness within. Breath is always there, wherever we go, whatever we do, or not do. One does not need any instructions. Nothing. Breath accompanies us, playing the music of life. This realization changed the way I breathed and meditated and lived. The three were not separate any more, but intertwined. It was not only my breath; in fact, there is no such thing as my breath. There is breath, and that's all. Wherever I turned, I saw plants, trees, animals and birds breathing and absorbing the air, and returning it back to nature. We were all breathing the same air; we were synchronized. The space between us was an illusion. The breath united us as it travelled from one being to another, adding something to it and taking something away from it. It was like magic!

From breath, I moved on to my body—the two were not separate, anyway.

Breath now became a tool to examine the body. Rather, it was a set of tools: a torch with which I could probe inside, an indicator to evaluate the state of my health, an aid to heal my body and mind, and much more. Every part of us, even our mind, is touched by breath. Once I focused on breath, listened to it, developed control over it, my body responded and found the missing parts of the puzzle. It was like a union. The union of my being. The sensation of breath going up and down my body, making every cell dance to its music—that revelation changed my perception of life. The exuberance of life, both inside and out, was hard to ignore. It happened effortlessly. So, when I worked on breath, it became clear to me that I was working on our entire existence. I wasn't specifically aiming at different aspects of my being, but I could no longer keep them out of this process. I tried different postures to guide my body in a way that I could experience this union.

Wherever I needed help, I sought Adi and there he was. Such are his ways. Every time I hope to see him, I get to see him. He does not tell me how that happens, nor do I ever ask. Perhaps he is always around, growing and glowing in the wild. One day, when I asked him about the secret to be one with the universe, he said that it was simple. Do not sit, stand, eat, work against the nature of the universe, but align yourself with it. He would look at the sky and the earth, and guide me to align my body accordingly.

'How do I align my body with the universe?' I asked him when he mentioned the secret.

'With upright body, head and neck, lead the mind and its powers into your heart. Make the sound of your breath your armour against all distractions, fears and anxieties. And when the body is in silent steadiness, breathe rhythmically through the nostrils with a peaceful ebbing and flowing of breath.'

It dawned upon me—breath is the key to life. When you are aware of your breath, you seize the moment.

The birds and animals had gathered around us as Adi explained this to me. It was as if a circus event was going on, with the roles being reversed, of course. They looked on curiously as we worked on different postures. They chittered and chattered, chirped, whispered, some even howled and roared. I was pretty sure what they were saying. They were saying: Why do humans do things that they don't have to?

Such silly beings. Still, they looked amused as if they were thanking us for the entertainment.

'What do I do with my thoughts?' I asked Adi when I found myself getting distracted and talking to the birds.

'Let them go,' he said. 'If they don't come back, fine, and if they do, perhaps nobody else wanted them.' He laughed and so did I.

'Wouldn't it be inappropriate to ask your guests to leave?'

'Not if the guest has sneaked in without your permission.'

'Are you sure?' I said, cheekily.

He laughed shook his head. 'I know what you mean,' he said.

I took a deep breath and let my thoughts go, and all of a sudden, the chatter died down. The more I practised, the quieter it got.

The breath, the postures, the alignment of the body and mind with the universe—they seem simple but they are all too powerful. Geometry is not only a field of study but a path to experience. It holds the key to the door that stands between the known and the unknown. Through this practice, my body was changing slowly, I could see it.

'I feel good about myself, as if I am twenty again,' I told Adi.

'There is something that you will have to remember at every step,' he said. 'We are not doing this only for the body. We are doing this to free ourselves.'

I listened intently.

'No doubt this will give you good health, lightness of body, awareness of emotions, absence of greedy desires, but this cannot be your end goal. Otherwise, you will get stuck in this forever. Liberation lies in breaking this cycle.'

I sat there like a child, eager to know more. Once I understood that the physical movements were not in any way separate from the soul and were only its manifestations, it became clear. I felt more connected with every part of me as well as every part of the outside world.

'Even a man who is asleep, awakens. You will wake up. It will take time, but you will . . . We may not know this, but a messenger comes to us if we follow the right path,' he would say and leave. Every time he left, I would feel that I had just woken up from a dream. Maybe, it was a dream. Maybe, he was my messenger.

Soon, I found the truth in his words. The more I looked within, the more I experienced it. My body could be a window to the unreal—I would have never imagined this.

With each passing day, I felt more awakened, as if I was beginning to get out of a deep slumber. The veil of what we call reality was slowly coming off. I felt as though I had been sleepwalking all along. The whole experience unshackled me. My fears began to wither away, one by one.

'What is the role of the body if we are seeking spiritual freedom?' I asked Adi.

He smiled, took a long pause to reflect and answered.

'What would you do if I asked you to cross a river? Would you walk or swim? You would swim, right? If you do not know swimming, what would you do? You would probably get a boat, isn't it? In either case, you would need a process, a tool. Without that, it is unlikely that you would make your journey. The same is true for a spiritual journey. Your body is the most reliable tool that you have. If you make good use of it, then you could go far.'

'You mean there are other ways too?'

'There are as many ways as you can imagine. But you don't have to imagine. Your path is yours. That is what you have. Simply focus on it.'

'What do I have to do to make progress?'

'Practise. Practise and you will wake up,' he would say at the end of every conversation. Sometimes when I bombarded Adi with a barrage of questions, he would simply smile and say this word. 'Practise.'

And that is what I did. I practised. The next few days involved only this and nothing else. Somewhat paradoxically, I discovered the path to freedom through an intense discipline. Each day has been more liberating than the previous one. I am slowly waking up.

Today, I am walking downhill. Not towards the cave, but on the other side. Adi has told me about a village where I could learn a few things that would help me in my journey. I look around. There is fresh green on this side of the valley. Since this is the first time in the last few weeks that I have left the woods, I feel a little warm as I descend. I have the comfort of basking in the glory of Surya, the sun god.

The snow is disappearing and the streams are gushing forth in a hurry. The valley seems to have transformed compared to the last time I was here. The shade of a tree feels invaluable during this time of the year. I look up and down, hoping to find a place to rest. I feel thirsty too. So, I walk to a nearby stream, bend forward, and drink directly with my mouth. I have acquired the ways of my fellow beings! I, too, am now a forest-dweller.

I hear a melodious voice. Could it be a woman saying something? I turn to see who is there.

She is sitting by a pool of water, holding a white flower in her hands and breathing in its fragrance. I don't know what she is trying to do, but I find the sight captivating. She has cupped the flower in her hand, her feet dipped in the water. The water is clear and I can see some colourful pebbles lying at the bottom. When there is a disturbance, I cannot see the pebbles clearly. Isn't it like our mind? How are we unable to look at the beautiful underlying reality in the chaos of everyday life? I stand and look at it for a few minutes. She suddenly notices that her solitude has been encroached upon.

'I am sorry; I did not know you were here,' she says and puts the flower down.

'Well, here I am,' I say with a smile.

'Maya,' she says, and walks up to me. She presents me with a firm handshake and says 'Hello.'

'Hello. I am Jeet,' I say as I shake her hand.

'Good to see you, Jeet. So, what are you doing here?'

'I should be asking you this question. I have been here for . . . well, you would have guessed from my beard.'

She laughs and says, 'Good point.'

'So, what brings you here?'

'I am just travelling. It's more than travelling, actually. I have been doing some research.'

'That sounds intriguing. Well, I am glad to have met you.'

'Thank you.'

'So what kind of research has brought you here, if I may ask?'

'Well, I have been studying and working in the field of neuroscience, in France. To cut a long story short, my research is broadly around the subject of consciousness.'

'It's very interesting that you came all the way here to research something that you would have found in the comfort of your home.'

She smiles sheepishly and says, 'I know. I wouldn't have imagined myself coming here for this. I have heard a lot about the mystics, and, you know, gurus, who live in these parts and have a unique understanding of consciousness. That was my reason. So far, I have met a few of them, but . . . I don't think I have made much progress.'

'Ah! So that's why you were connecting with the flower's consciousness, eh?'

'You got me there,' she says and glances at the flower. 'But hey, come on. I am pretty sure that flowers are not conscious beings.'

'Are you really sure about that? What if the flower wants to disagree?'

'Well, *it* surely can,' she smiles. 'But . . . I can only speak from my own limited understanding and what my research has taught me. Based on that I would say that consciousness emerges in evolved species such as ourselves, not plants. The question is, how?'

'And how far have you come to answering that question?'

'I don't know. It seems like such a mystery. I am very sure, though, that we will solve this puzzle. The scientific community, I mean. The whole concept of it is fascinating. Not just to the scientists but the philosophers as well.'

'That's interesting. So, tell me, what does this mean in scientific terms, this consciousness?'

'Umm . . . Let me try. If I were to explain it to you in simple words, I would say, what is it like to feel something? We often use the example of a bat. American philosopher Thomas Nagel framed this question: What is it like to be a bat? Sure, objectively we can define all the features and qualities of a bat, but there is a subjective element to being a bat as well. Like if I tell you the frequency of a colour, it makes no difference to your personal experience of looking at that colour. That subjective, first-hand experience is what we call consciousness.'

'I don't see a problem there, in its understanding.'

'The problem comes when we go deeper. I mean, the study of the brain and different psychological states, these are still easier problems, relatively speaking. But the difficult problem is . . . how do I say it? Really difficult.'

'What is that?'

'The difficult problem is to explain where the subjective feelings come from. To explain phenomenal consciousness, in other words. How can consciousness arise from non-conscious objects? That's the challenging question to unravel.'

'That sounds like an uphill task . . . it probably explains why you are up here,' I say, laughing. 'What makes you think that science can measure or quantify consciousness?'

'Science measures anything that is quantifiable. There is no other reliable way. I know what you are suggesting, but then, if we continue on that path, we can find all kinds of crazy and bizarre answers that have no rational basis. You know, this man I met on my travels—he told me that we are possessed by ghosts and death is the only way to get any sanity. Human imagination can go really far, you see.'

'But I am asking a different question. I am asking, how do we know consciousness is quantifiable? That it can be reduced to physical systems?'

'What other possibilities are there? Do you mean there is some kind of magic at work?'

'I am just asking a question,' I say and offer a few berries. She accepts.

'Hmm. Let me think about it,' she says. 'Thanks for these, by the way. I hope these are not conscious.'

'Ha ha. Let's just sit here,' I say, as I sit down on a small rock. 'Even if they were conscious, they don't have physical organs as we do, to feel pain in the same way.'

'You are right,' she says and sits next to me. 'I mean, I get your point. If consciousness were not quantifiable, then this approach may not be helpful. But frankly, I don't think that is the case. Think about it this way: either consciousness exists or it does not exist. There cannot be any other option. If it exists, then we should be able to measure it. We know it exists as a consequence of the evolutionary progress of life on earth. There is almost consensus in the scientific community over this. That our consciousness came out of material evolution.'

'For that you will have to assume that the material world exists outside our consciousness. Quite honestly, that is a big assumption.'

'Ah! That old puzzle. If a tree falls in a forest and no one is around to hear it, does it make a sound?'

'I know another one . . . if a husband says something in the woods and his wife is not there, is he still wrong?'

'Jungle humour?' she asks.

We both laugh and look around. There is a pause. Perhaps she is waiting for me to answer.

'I mean,' I take a deep breath as I muster the courage to answer this question intelligently, 'the only thing that we can confidently say that exists is consciousness.

There can be doubts when it comes to the material world, based on human capabilities, our perception, etc. I mean, you and I could be in a dream right now, but this experience, what we are feeling right now, we cannot deny that, can we?'

'Let me make it more challenging for you. Where is the evidence?'

'It's the only thing for which you don't need any evidence. Evidence needs a conscious being, not the other way around. You know it. You know that you exist. The rest of the world might be an illusion. But this is one thing that you know is true beyond evidence. Because any evidence that you are going to seek, whether you find it or not, is going to happen with you as an observer. Without your subjective observation, it won't be possible.'

'You don't think we can understand consciousness by studying the brain?'

'Unlikely. The life of computers and machines is in binaries. Sadly, these days, many humans behave that way too. Either right or wrong. Either this or that. But the truth is neither this nor that, it's something else. This dualistic perspective makes us more and more machine-like. The question is, how can we stop living like machines? Stop seeing everything as ones and zeroes? How can we create awareness of oneness and interconnection?'

'I understand what you are saying. But, coming back to the point of consciousness, what is it really? Can we define it? Understand it?'

'You can try defining it by using an equation, but it won't work. A better way is to understand it by yourself.'

'But how does one believe it?'

'Now you sound like a believer.'

'No way,' she laughs.

'Belief is when you don't experience it. Only then do you require it. For example, to accept that there can be matter without consciousness is a big claim that requires belief, not experience. Because without consciousness, there can be no experience of matter.'

'My fear is that when you go off the objective track, all you are left with is subjective experience, which, of course, cannot be measured scientifically. So what happens there is that anybody can make any claim about the reality and we cannot verify it. Whose version is true? We will never know.'

'I think you are confusing subjective experience with personal experience. Subjective experience can be universal, such as in the case of consciousness. It doesn't have to be personal in every case.'

'What is this consciousness then, according to you?'

'Consciousness is what permeates everything in our universe. There is nothing like your consciousness or my consciousness; there is only consciousness. You and I are only reflecting it through our physical systems. Think of it as multiple glasses being filled with water from a stream. Surely different glasses or different surfaces can contain different amounts of water, but that does not mean that water is only restricted to one or a few glasses. Water exists independent of its containers.

Similarly, everything and everyone around us is filled with consciousness and is reflecting it according to its physical nature. That does not mean consciousness has its limits. Consciousness is not restricted to my body or yours. It is not restricted to the wakeful state. When you dream, you are conscious. And when you are in deep sleep, you are conscious there too. It is what lies beyond wakefulness.'

'I suppose we both have a different understanding of consciousness. But, I will think more about your ideas. You know, my mind keeps going back to the rational concept, and that is why it won't be satisfied until I see some evidence.'

'If you assume that consciousness can emerge out of intelligence, wouldn't computers be conscious?'

'They might be . . . in the future.'

'Why in the future? Our neurons are much slower than the computer systems that we have today. A million times slower, at least.'

'That's a fair point. I will give you that.'

'The important question is, can you find any evidence outside of your consciousness?'

'That is impossible, by definition. That's the main challenge in understanding this.'

'You don't have to understand, but experience.'

She laughs and looks away. 'What do I have to do for that?'

'Just breathe.'

She smiles and takes a deep breath. I look at her and then at the sky behind. It looks ominous and is getting covered with dark clouds. Soon the clouds roar and begin to take rebirth in the form of rain. I look at myself and wonder if the same is happening within me.

'Let's go,' Maya says, as she runs to take cover. I look up. The raindrops are falling on my face. They are like breath too, connecting the heavens and the earth, and transforming whatever they touch. Everything is like breath. Everything is a part of me.

Chapter 4

Forgotten Secrets

Walking through the narrow lanes of the village with stone houses on either side, I get a sense of déjà vu. *I have been here*, I wonder, *but when*? Maybe not the exact same house, lane or village, but in human civilization, where man-made structures obstruct the union of the heaven and earth. This feels familiar. I remember meandering through a concrete jungle during lunch breaks at my office, trying to look for the horizon. That was a long time ago. Now that I am here, it feels as if I am travelling back in time. I take a moment to pause and see what surrounds me.

Every place preserves memories of its own past; these lanes, criss-crossing at every corner, tell the stories of generations of human activity. The houses are thoughtfully constructed, leaving enough space for gardens, yards, animal shelters, drains and sewers.

The stones, dark-grey in colour, are taken from a nearby hill (probably carried by people from previous generations on their shoulders) and stacked upon each other, leaving no gaps in between; if there was any, it was filled with smaller stones. The stone pavements also tell similar stories; stories of people—living or dead—they have carried upon themselves, thereby sinking deeper into the ground. The air has a distinct scent, not that of the wild, but of domesticity. I can smell the presence of cattle, fused with burning incense. There is smoke too; the fire, I cannot see yet. As I walk further, I hear human chatter coming from the next street and . . . a fascinating sight awaits me as soon as I reach the end of the lane.

A few people have gathered to form a circle. Their collective chants stir my curiosity. I hurry and wade through the crowd, and make my way to the centre. Finally, I can see what is going on. A little boy is crying in the middle. He cries as he looks down and finds more strands of hair falling next to him, some on the ground and some on his bare feet. A man, holding him by his shoulder, is shaving the boy's head with an old razor. He murmurs something every time the razor moves on his head. This is followed by a loud chant from the small crowd. Two women, one considerably old and one younger, are praying to a deity, with hands folded and eyes closed. A little girl is clasping the young woman by her sari and is trying to imitate every gesture of hers. These five—appearing to be of one family—are sitting cross-legged on the ground and are surrounded by a group of a dozen or so people (now I am among them as well), standing in a circle and chanting. Unable to make sense of what these words mean, I simply move my lips and raise my hands as everyone else. The little girl is amused to see the crowd chanting and jumps in excitement. The little boy sits disheartened. Another patch gets removed, and another tear rolls down his cheek. The chanting grows intense. The sounds resonate, the smoke rises into the sky.

What is going on? I try to remember.

I think of the time when I was in rural China. The village was such that all its inhabitants followed millennia-old practices in most aspects of their lives. Life was simple, as it should be; sometimes hard, but simple. Separated from the rest of the world for most of the year, the villagers consumed little from outside; mostly what they grew and what they made out of it. They embraced the customs passed on to them from their ancestors and shared stories from the past. It was in that place that I first learnt to see the beauty in ancient traditions.

There, it was a norm to trim the hair of an infant. They would do it after the first month, on the day of the full moon. It was an act of gratitude, a remembrance of those who had lived before them and were no longer there, especially infants who could not survive to see the next phases of their life. There was a time when the infant mortality rate was very high in those regions. If the child survived for one month, people thought that the worst was behind them and there was every chance that the child would live on; hence, the celebrations. The tradition continued. The villagers had told me that they would make a brush using the child's first hair and it would be preserved throughout its life. The brush would serve as a reminder that life is precious and one must value it above all else. Similar traditions exist in many other regions across the world. A child's first haircut, or a certain haircut during its developing years, is considered sacred.

Why does hair get such importance in different cultures? I ponder as I see the ceremony taking place before me.

Hair forms an interesting part of one's identity. You can shed it off without having to go through any pain. That may also be true for nails, but nails do not form such a key part of our appearance, particularly our face, which is central to our identity in the physical world. So, when you shave your hair, you accept a change. You look different, feel different, as if you have transitioned into a new person. It has a deep psychological impact while moving from one stage of life to another. Accepting change then becomes easy. That is why many religious and cultural traditions recommend this practice on important occasions; the occasions may vary from birth to puberty, or even death. The ritual, performed in the presence of other people, adds strength to your conviction. Your belief grows manifold. The same is true for other rituals, performed during other life events. Not all of them may make sense right away, but when you think deeply, you see the point.

I pay more attention to the ceremony now. This boy is a little older than the one I saw in China; perhaps around two or three. The idea, an old man informs me, is to cleanse the child from the sins of previous births.

'One carries a lot of baggage from the past; at some point one has to drop it,' he says. 'If you don't, it brings new troubles.'

'How do you drop it? With a razor?'

'Oh yes, not just drop it but raze it to the ground. Finish it completely,' he says, dramatically. 'And that razor you see, it is not an ordinary one. It was passed on to us from our ancestors,' he folds his hands in reverence as he mentions the last word. 'It is meant specially for these purposes.'

'I like the idea of . . . razing the past to the ground. It's powerful imagery,' I say. I am not sure if he gets my point, but he continues.

'These sins come in the form of hair from previous births. I have seen some kids with bear-like hair. This long,' he laughs and stretches his hands. 'God only knows what they did back in time. Hair, I tell you. It is a sign of the past, the mistakes one made there. It can continue to grow in this birth as well. That is the reason it is supposed to be removed.'

'Hair today and gone tomorrow!' I say, smiling and shaking my head, thinking that he may not have understood the wordplay. 'I cannot say much on this matter but I find the explanation very interesting.'

'Yes, this is the mechanism we have adopted over generations.'

That is another thing about rituals, I realize. There is always a story woven around a logical explanation. When a story changes, it evolves; when logic changes, it collapses. So, if one were to choose between the two, the former is a much better choice. Stories are powerful, they stand the test of time. These stories may vary—as it was different in China—but the underlying ideas remain the same. A story travels quickly and smoothly and goes further than any scientific explanation. More importantly, it is easier to pass on to the subsequent generations—one only has to untangle the story to extract the real meaning out of it. A story, therefore, is an amalgamation of generations of human effort. It speaks and absorbs and travels—it is alive. Much like we are.

A ritual, on the other hand, is not merely restricted to its story; it is an 'act', and therefore, as much about how you perform it as about the idea itself. Rituals bring people closer, forge new bonds, develop convictions and leave a lasting impact on one's psyche. To think about a ritual is to reflect on our nature, sociality and culture. It is not only limited to humans—animals engage in rituals too. Honeybees, for example, perform a series of abdominal waggles and footwork upon returning to the hive after nectar-gathering. The bee dances while others observe it. That is their ritual. Humans have their own; sometimes we are aware of them, sometimes not. For example, your hand reaching out to your phone when you hear a notification—you may not call it a ritual, but you perform it like one.

'Wow!' I watch in awe as the people chant prayers, their hands pointing to the sky.

The man conducting the ritual looks at me and smiles once he finishes. The boy, now bald and shiny-headed, is not crying any more as he is being offered sweets along with some gifts. He wipes his tears and laughs, as everyone around him laughs and claps. They sing songs of praises and pat his back as they disperse. The little girl runs towards the boy and tries to touch his newly revealed head. 'So soft,' she says and slaps it. He feels slightly embarrassed and shrugs it off. Now, the family turns their attention towards me. Their stares have a lot of questions, I can see that. I stand in front of them not knowing what to say or do.

'Hello,' I say. The kids respond with a shy 'Hello', while the adults nod their heads with a friendly demeanour.

The old woman points at me and says something that I cannot comprehend. The man interrupts her and speaks to me in my language.

'She is asking you to have food with us,' he tells me. 'You are a guest and we welcome you in our village. Come with us, let's eat.'

'As you say,' I oblige, and smile at the old woman. She smiles back and waves at me.

'Come now,' the man says and leads me towards the yard. 'I am Shakti.'

'Jeet. Thank you for offering me food.'

'There is no shortage of food today,' he laughs and I laugh too.

We sit on the ground cross-legged, and turn to the food being served on a large leaf. I pick up a piece of bread; the ash on its surface tells me that it was cooked in an earthen stove. What else would they cook in, in these mountains anyway? The vegetables are locally grown, which I would not have found elsewhere. There is also sweet milk on offer, only a few spoonfuls unfortunately. From its taste, I get a sense that it could be goat milk. Everyone eats, drinks milk, and no one utters a word during this time. I observe their faces, one by one. They all look like relatives to me: freckled faces, red cheeks, almost similar body structures. They eat patiently—no one seems to be in a hurry.

Everyone finishes the food served on the leaf; nothing remains. Even the leaves would be fed to the livestock. The ancient way of living puts hardly any pressure on nature and makes the life cycle much more sustainable. I am reminded of a story I read in a magazine last year while sitting in the comfort of the sofa in my home. It said that one-third of the food is wasted every year, and that amount is growing. I wonder if we could take a leaf out of these people's book (quite literally) and rearrange our priorities.

'Adi sent me here,' I say, once we have finished the food. 'I thought I should mention that.'

'You don't have to. I know this already,' Shakti says.

'How did you know? Do you know him?'

'Everyone does. He is famous in these parts.'

'Did he come here and tell you about me?'

'Yes, yes. Who else could send you here? He is the only one who could do that. He comes here and then wanders off. He walks on the snow as he always has . . . my son has named him snowman. He chases the snowman by following his gigantic footprints. But the snowman is out of sight by then; he is never out of mind, though.'

I smile. 'What else did he tell you?' I ask.

'Not much,' he shrugs his shoulders. 'He says very little. He comes and goes and lets the others say what they wish to say. That is why he has already become a part of the folklore. Too much mystery there. We have invited him to stay with us, but he comes and goes as he pleases. Maybe he feels the mountains are his home. I wish he could visit us more often.'

'That would be wonderful,' I say in agreement.

After a moment of silence, we turn back and watch the little boy walk across the yard. He seems to cherish the fact that the party is over.

'Look at him,' Shakti says. 'He already looks healthier. He is going to get better now. For the last few months, he was not listening to us, not eating well, not focusing on anything. He would get annoyed at the smallest of things. His health was affected too—he would fall ill often. But I am happy now. He will get better. Don't you think?'

'Yes,' I say. That's the only word I could think of.

I have some questions, but I stay silent. Sometimes it is a good idea to let people believe what they believe; sometimes it is the only support they have. Killing a belief could be worse than killing a human being. When you kill a human, you take their life, but when you take their faith, they are left without hope, without meaning. That is hell, in the truest sense.

'I am so fortunate to have such a great family,' he says, as he introduces me to them. 'The five of us live here. My mother, we call her Amma. Ganga, my wife. Mehak, my daughter—she has just turned nine. She is a very good girl. And this is Aakash, my three-year-old son. It's his day, today.'

'Nice to meet you all,' I say and smile. They all smile back. The boy, Aakash, looks at me shyly and tries to cover his newly shaved head with his hands.

'Adi told me that you needed to stay for a week. However, you are welcome to stay here with us for as long as you wish,' Shakti says.

'Thank you,' I say, as we enter the house.

I don't understand why Adi said that, but then, who could understand him? He had told me that I needed to learn a few things in this village. 'Observe, and absorb,' he had said. 'This is your fate and you should accept it.' And so, I did.

It is after a long time that I find myself inside the confines of a room. I feel odd; the four walls seem intrusive. The family has offered me some clothes and a quilt and that feels slightly odd to my body. I marvel at the body's ability to adjust to new conditions. *I will try to connect to this place as well. Let me observe and absorb*, I tell myself and enter the realm of the other world by shutting the windows of my eyes. I drift away into a deep slumber.

The family's life is simple. They wake up before the morning sun and take to their jobs. Shakti goes out to the fields and collects wood. He also brings some vegetables and fruits with him. Then, he tends to the cattle. His wife Ganga, after she has finished her chores, brings water from a nearby stream. By the time the sun shows up, she serves tea to everyone, and starts preparing the first meal of the day. She is always busy doing one thing or another, never taking a break. Amma mostly prays or looks after the children during the morning hours. I think of Adi and thank him in gratitude. It's only because of him that I could spend time with this wonderful family.

There is no school in the village, or anywhere close. The kids learn whatever they can learn in this remote place. The entire community comes together and makes use of all the tools they have at their disposal. Mostly, they pass on the ancestral wisdom to the younger lot or allow kids to learn by themselves, which is very different from schooling. It does not mean that people are uneducated here. In fact, it's silly to say that anyone, anywhere, is uneducated. People get educated in different ways; some at home, some in the wilderness, some in playgrounds, some during tragedies, some while listening to the stories of their grandparents, and some at school. It's unfortunate that we only use the tag of 'educated' for those who enrol in factory-like institutions. In fact, a child with only school education is an uneducated child; they might know all the calculations but might still struggle in life.

The family is happy in their own small world and does not fancy the pleasures of modernity. They are all usually smiling through the day. If one looks without any prejudice, one would find that they are living a good life. Not a life of great comfort, but a good life, nevertheless.

'Are you happy?' Ganga asks everyone at the end of the day. She goes to each member of the family and asks this question. If she senses there is something that can cause unhappiness, she discusses the matter and tries to find the solution collectively. It is such a simple, yet profound way to connect with family.

'Are you happy?' she asks me, once they have discussed family matters. I can see that she doesn't ask this only for the sake of asking; she genuinely means it.

'I haven't asked myself this question in a while, but now that you have asked, I definitely feel happy,' I say. She smiles and offers her gratitude to the almighty.

'Son, if you look after others' health, your own health improves,' Amma adds.

Suddenly, faced with such a basic, yet satisfying question, I feel a sense of privilege.

Privilege. It's a term that we often associate with material benefits. When we see a rich man, we call him privileged. There might be some truth in that, but I believe there is a lot more to life. It makes me think. There are numerous privileges available to us. Being able to take a nap in the afternoon is a privilege, watching the sunset is a privilege, sharing a room with your grandmother and listening to her stories is a privilege, living close to nature and breathing fresh air is a privilege, someone showing concern about your happiness is a privilege. Owning an ornament made of a rare metal is a privilege too, but it does not seem as valuable when compared to some of these other privileges. We don't realize this, but often those whom we call privileged deny themselves the simple pleasures available to humanity.

I marvel at the simplicity of their lives as I think about all this.

'Are you happy?' I ask Amma first, and then the other members of the family. This is a lesson that I am going to carry with me for the rest of my life.

Another thing I have noticed about the family is that they are completely engrossed in the task at hand. If they are cooking, they talk about cooking; if they are cleaning, they talk about cleaning. They stay rooted to where they are and don't let their minds wander too far.

So, now that we are about to have supper, Amma starts talking to me about food.

'Eat food like you would eat medicine,' she says. 'How do you take a medicine? You see what is in it, you think what it will do to your body, and you are mindful of its effects. Do that with food as well. Eat food like a medicine.'

It gets me thinking.

Shakti and Ganga smile. They smile a lot, especially Ganga. When she looks at her children, she smiles; when she talks to Shakti or Amma, she smiles. It is almost impossible to imagine her face without a smile.

'So, we have to be on medicine all the time,' I quip, raising my eyebrows. Amma starts laughing.

'Eat for yourself, not for your doctor. Otherwise he will get very rich,' she says and laughs again.

'Yes, there is a lot of wisdom in what you are saying, Amma. What kind of medicine are you on, if I may ask?'

'Ha ha. I am on the strongest drug. For me, the presence of these children is the medication that god has prescribed,' she says.

'I know what you mean. You can either be sad or be with a child.'

'But you can be troubled. Let's see if you see any troubles in it,' she says, as we call it a night.

Only in the morning do I realize what Amma meant by those troubles. I have been assigned the job of the babysitter for the day, and I have to look after two. The girl, Mehak, talks endlessly; her brother, Aakash, is quiet, but he just cannot sit still. Looking after both of them in the same room is a task that I did not think would test the success of my meditations. When I turn to attend to one, the other starts to burn the house down. It goes on for a while, until complete chaos takes over. How do I give undivided attention to both of them at the same time? I come up with a plan.

'I have a challenge for you. Let's play a game of poses. Try a Superman pose like this,' I say.

Mehak gets up, but Aakash hesitates. I pick him up and make him stand. 'Be like Superman.' He smiles and poses.

'Now try a Wonder Woman pose.'

This time, they follow my words with curiosity on their faces. Neither knows anything about these superheroes, but how does that matter? That's the beauty of childhood. We all jump together now.

'Now,' I clap to grab their attention, 'let's go a step further and sharpen our senses like wild animals. You like wild animals, don't you? The leopards, the bears, the wolves, right? Let's pretend to be like one of them and use our smelling power. What do you smell here, close to the window?'

The three of us crawl on the floor and pretend to sniff.

'There is a smell of flowers, of trees, and?'

'Soil?' Mehak says.

'Good. Now tell me, what do you smell near the door?'

'Food,' both yell, one by one.

'Now let's do the sounds,' I say, pointing at my ears. 'What do you hear? Tell me all the sounds.'

'Birds,' Mehak says, at the top of her voice.

'What else?'

'That is a goat. Now Amma is saying something. Now . . .'

'Tell me more.'

'There is your voice. Now, someone is cleaning utensils in the kitchen.'

'And there is the sound of breath. Let's be quiet and hear it. Do you hear it?'

'Yes,' they whisper, one by one.

'Very well. Now look for colours. Tell me as many as you can find.'

'White, green, blue,' says Mehak, looking through the window.

'Yellow,' says Aakash.

'What colour is this sheet?'

'Red,' they both say together.

'And what is this?' I ask Aakash, pointing at his shirt.

'This is pink,' he says.

'Well done! Being mindful of your surroundings, feeling things around you, isn't it wonderful?' I say. 'You should play this game every day.'

It all turns out well, only that at the end of the day I have a headache. Ouch! It hurts. Clearly, I have a lot to learn on the subject of babysitting. Shakti notices me sitting with my head in my hands.

'Do you have a hammer or something?'

He stands there and laughs.

'Like a painkiller?'

'Let me tell you something, Jeet. Taking these modern medicines for a headache is like arming a cannon to kill a mosquito. It is effective, no doubt, but often unnecessary. Why would you drive down to your neighbour's house when you could just walk across the road?'

It makes sense to me. Why did it never occur to me all these years? Now that I think about it, many of my efforts seem to have been wasted in the light of this simple question. My rational brain still has some doubts, but I know in my heart that there is truth in what he is saying.

'Should I not take a medicine?' I ask.

'You could. But unfortunately, we don't have these medicines. Besides, medicines kill the symptoms of a disease; often they do not eliminate the cause. That is something we should work on, fixing the cause of the problem. Try to follow the path of what triggered the illness. Once you have the answer, you will find the cure as well. You may then have to take a medicine or you may have to perform some activity, but in that case, you will only kill the mosquito, and not bomb the entire house. The body is its own doctor. Just restore the balance in your body and it will heal itself.'

'Thank you . . . but what should I do now?'

'Let me check,' he says and puts his hand on my forehead. 'Does it hurt here?'

'No, it hurts at the back of my head.'

'I see. I will give you a drink. That should help,' he says, and goes into the kitchen. His wife is already there, chopping vegetables for supper. She smiles as he enters and the two start talking. Once again, a lot of smiles are being exchanged along with words and gestures. Then, he strokes her hair and she blushes.

'Please take it,' Shakti says, when he comes out and hands the drink to me. It is hot and tastes terrible.

'Don't worry,' says Ganga, who has just walked out of the kitchen. 'The headache will go away in no time. And you can get back to playing with the kids.'

'I look forward to it,' I say with a worried look on my face. I drink every drop of the concoction as the couple watches me keenly.

Now that I see the two, it makes me think of my wife. I wonder what she is doing, how much she is missing my presence. It must have been hard for her—letting me go. But, she knows how much I was seeking, how restless I felt back at home. She understands. That is the great quality she has; she always understands.

Suddenly, I feel a longing to see her. That face, that smile, that gentle touch. At the same time, I also know that my journey has just begun. It will take time. I feel a deep sense of gratitude towards my wife. *Thank you*, I whisper. What is this saltiness I feel in my mouth? I suddenly realize, tears have rolled down and found their way to my lips.

Another day has gone by. I go to bed early, still thinking about my family. What is my wife thinking at this hour? What is my son doing? What is my mother saying? Do they miss me? Are they happy? So many thoughts cross my mind. Thoughts of my family, friends, the familiar faces—I feel overwhelmed.

I close my eyes and think of Adi. I see him in the village, living in the same house. It must be a dream; it is a dream.

The morning wakes me up with apocalyptic battle cries. It's only the brother and sister, and they are running around, throwing things at each other. Amma scolds.

'Why are you fighting?' she asks in a loud voice.

'Why?' the boy says too.

'Why?' the girl repeats. They both laugh hysterically.

Amma decides to get up now. It takes some effort but she finds a way. She grabs the little boy by his hand

and brings him to the bed. She makes him and his sister sit there.

'First of all, you will have to stop shouting,' Amma says.

'Why?' the girl says, and her brother repeats.

'You shout when someone is very far. Have you seen—when people get angry, they shout?'

'Yes.'

'That's because when they get angry, their hearts grow distant. So, they have to shout.'

'Oh, that is why they shout. I didn't know that.'

'Now you know. And you should also know that you two need to help each other and not fight.'

'Why?' the girl says.

'Do you not remember that story?'

'Which story?'

'That of the crow, deer, rat and tortoise.'

'Please tell that story again, Amma.'

'Please, Amma,' cries the boy too.

'Okay, okay, here goes. Once upon a time, there were four friends. A crow, a deer, a rat and a tortoise. They always helped each other, especially in difficult situations as there were many such situations in the forest. One day, a hunter came to the forest. On seeing the hunter, the crow flew to the highest branch of a tree. The deer ran into the woods. The rat hid in a hole. The tortoise was slow, so the hunter caught him and put him in a bag. The three friends were distraught and wanted to save their friend. So, they hatched a plan. The crow flew up to locate the hunter. Once located, the deer ran past him and pretended to be dead, and as the hunter ran to chase the deer, the rat opened the bag and released their friend, the tortoise. When the hunter reached the deer, it sprang up and ran away. The hunter went back and found the tortoise missing. He realized that he should not have been greedy. The four friends went back to the forest and lived happily.'

'I like this story,' Mehak says.

'That is why you should help each other,' Amma says. 'Did you learn something from the story?'

'Yes.'

'What lesson did you learn from the story?'

'That we should not be greedy and help each other,' Mehak says.

'A flower may bloom in a pot, but it blooms more beautifully in a garden. The same is with people. More so when it comes to family and friends. Look after them when they are in need.'

'Yes, we will.'

'Listen, girl. You are older than your brother. You should understand this. He will understand it too, but give him some time. Now, listen carefully. One day, I will leave you, and so will your parents. But you two, brother and sister, will spend a lot of years together while growing up and later, until the end of your lives. So, better learn to live with each other. And don't fight, okay?'

'Okay.'

'Do you understand?' she asks lovingly.

'Yes, I do.'

'And you, little boy, do you understand too?'

'Yes, you understand too.'

We all laugh. The feeling of 'I' has not been imprinted on his mind yet.

The brother and sister start playing once again. This time, there is hardly any animosity; there is much more love . . . How simple advice can change lives!

The week goes by, in the blink of an eye. *Time is so relative*, it gets me thinking. One moment, I had arrived here, and it seems, the next moment, I am about to go back. The cave awaits me.

I have learnt so many things from this family. I have learnt how traditional values, when preserved in the form of stories, carry profound wisdom in them; however, one needs to pay close attention. I have seen the happiness in relationships. I have seen the beauty in simplicity and living in true harmony with your community as well as nature. I have learnt how, if we all come together and help each other, our lives could improve radically.

As I look at them one last time before taking their leave, I see how, despite being different, they all complement and complete one another. They are like the five elements of our body: earth, fire, water, air and sky. Just like the five elements make us, these five made a family. Things go well when each element is devoted to the whole, not just its individual well-being. A family, if managed well, can be as lively as a human being. Perhaps, it too has a soul of its own, its own desires, life and death, who knows?

I feel a need for balance. Not in the same way as I had thought earlier. I feel the need of it in my own body, and outside of it too, in our families, societies, everywhere. If that balance gets disturbed, then we are troubled—a disease might occur, a family might fall apart, society might break down, the earth might lose its life. So much can happen. As long as we are able to maintain balance, we can be certain that life on earth will go on.

They all smile at me and wave with both their hands. I wave back. The family appears like a necklace to me, with each member like a bead tied to the other through a string of shared values. New beads will replace the old ones, but the necklace will remain, hopefully.

I wish this beautiful family goodbye with a heavy heart and hope to see them one more time. The cave is on the other side of the valley; it's going to be a long walk. I look up at the dark sky, the rains—they are here. I must hurry.

Chapter 5

Jewels in a Cave

On the first day, I waited eagerly.

I had gone up and down the hill, around the valley, drenched in rain and hoping to see Adi. By the time I reached, all soaked, it was already late. So, I waited until sunrise, which turned into noon and noon turned into evening; the day got away from me, not the excitement though. I had brought a flute from the village, which I hoped Adi would enjoy playing. 'Maybe he also has something in store for me: new stories, more wisdom, and above all, his presence.' I waited in anticipation. He wasn't around and I had been waiting; yet, I was brimming with hope and high spirits. The time spent between a desire and its possession is often exciting. The day seemed suspiciously short as I waited for Adi in excitement. My mind started imagining all kinds of scenarios that could take place once Adi would show up; things we would share and how we would sing and dance. The only problem was . . . he did not show up. The rain continued—sometimes sporadically, and then steadily, throughout the day and into the night, as I sat with eyes fixed on the entrance of the cave.

On the second day, the eagerness turned into inquiry. My mind, first taking eagerness for granted and then keeping it on the back shelf, started jumping around, playing tricks and asking different questions. Where is Adi? What is he doing? Why is he not showing up? Is he safe or is he in trouble? There were far too many questions than I could even begin to answer. My eagerness was being pulled back as I sensed my curiosity advancing, my mouth drying a little and my muscles feeling tense. As the day progressed, my thoughts kept going back to what Shakti and the other villagers had told me about Adi. 'He does not like to spend time with people,' they had said. 'He is a strange man, from some other world—god knows where.' That, and his continued absence, planted a seed of doubt in my mind. He wasn't around and I had been waiting, and now, the questions filled me with doubts. The doubts sprouted in all directions as water came seeping inside the cave. The rains, getting heavier with each passing moment, continued incessantly. I did not move from my spot; I did not want to move or blink my eyes. Maybe he was really a man of the wild who did not care about people. What if he was one? Who is he, really? Why do I care about him? That's the thing. I do. I don't know the reason, but I do. Maybe he had secrets that he would never reveal. It made me sceptical and I kept pondering over various possibilities, until I fell asleep late in the night.

On the third day, there was despair.

The despair made inroads, straddling my thoughts and strangling my hope; once inside, it refused to retreat. Now that it was here, it spread its roots in my mind. As the seed sprouted and bore fruits, fears and worries were the first ones to branch and spread. I could not make sense of it. Was I worried about Adi or myself in his absence? I saw no light; there wasn't much light, either. The dark clouds had been thundering and pouring all day long. The skies roared and the earth went mysteriously quiet. My ears went numb every time lightning struck in the valley. The lights were brighter than a thousand suns; the sounds louder than any explosion I had ever heard. But . . . none of that concerned me too much. My mind, taken over by anxiety, was roaming somewhere else. I could feel this sensation travelling through my body. Every part of it slowly got tense. The mind, too, felt vulnerable under this assault. Adi wasn't around and I was waiting, and the pain filled me. I was in utter despair. Why are you not coming? What has happened to you? I cried bucketloads, like a child who has been denied his favourite toy and who cannot wrap his head around such cosmic injustice. It was a feeling of helplessness. For the first time in all these months, I felt lonely. As if I was sitting in a distant planet. It can be frightening when you realize that you are truly lonely; there is no one around—it is you and only you in the whole world. I had been alone in the past as well, but fear had never stifled me the way it did that day. I felt my body, my mind, responding to the fear that had engulfed me. I was frozen. I did not feel hungry or thirsty. In that one day, where time barely moved, I experienced the suffering of a lifetime.

The fourth day seems different. All things pass and so has one of the longest days of my life.

The fourth day has woken me up with a surprise. I lie in the cave for some time, trying to make sense of the world around me. There is no more rain, no sign, no trace of it left. Birds are chirping, brooks are burbling forth. The sky has cleared and the morning rays have found their way into the cave and on to my face. I feel it in my gut that I need to eat—something I haven't done since I came back from the village. I am hungry; more importantly, I am aware that I am hungry—the first signs of life. My body feels weak as I stand and limp forward; the light is drawing me towards itself. The strength comes naturally. By the time I step out, I feel much better.

It has been three days, I tell myself and make my way towards the waterfall. The earth is damp and . . . the smell of fresh, damp earth—it is unlike any other in nature. After drinking water (and a lot of it), I gaze at the valley and its endless contours, spreading in every direction to meet the horizon. It is lush green everywhere. New streams have appeared; new life has emerged. I can see more insects on the ground, more birds in the sky. The sight, the smell, the sounds—they feel different today. I get immersed in them. It's a new world as far as I can tell. It's interesting how new seasons bring new sights and new emotions in our life. How a small change in scenery can bring such a huge transformation in our mindsets. Perhaps that is the reason, whenever there were demons in my head, I picked up the broom and started slaying them under the carpet. Strangely, it did feel better once the room was cleaned.

What is it that I feel today? To be honest, I don't know. When you are enjoying a moment, you don't have time to think. If you think, the moment gets away. But, when you are there, existing in the moment, you feel alive, you feel free. I don't know what is it that I feel today, but I am experiencing life as it should be experienced—without judgement, without prejudice. I forget all that has transpired and all that is about to come. There is this moment, with a window into the past and a door into the future. This is where we truly live.

I feel the bliss, and the moment that happens, guess who shows up?

He walks on the trail, right next to the waterfall, as I stand agape. Where does he come from and what does he return to? I wish to ask, but as it usually happens in his presence, words fail me. I do not ask any question, nor say a word. How can I? Even my words are taking his side. He enters the cave and I follow him shortly after.

There is enough light in the cave today. I can see him clearly. He sits cross-legged, and without bothering to exchange any words, closes his eyes.

Umm . . . what do I do? I sit on the opposite side, staring at him. Sometimes he brings music, sometimes silence. Maybe he is the music and he is the silence.

Now, he opens his eyes and looks at me. His eyes are wide open, unmoving and sparkling uninterruptedly. I have not seen anyone watching me this way before. I don't know what to say.

'What are you thinking?' he asks me.

'Nothing,' I say. Just like words, thoughts betray me too in his presence, but I grab hold of some and continue, 'Of late, there have been too many things on my mind. I don't know where to begin.'

'You don't have to,' he says. 'I know. You are a modern man, after all. How can I forget that? Thoughts take control. Emotions dictate. It's the gift bestowed upon the modern man. He lives by it and dies by it.'

'What do you mean?' I ask curiously.

'Let me tell you something. I have been here, wandering in these mountains for who knows how long. People from different times and places have come here and shared their stories with me. I will tell you about one such instance. There was a man who travelled with me in these parts for years. He was "the man with a fever", for he would always carry this fever with him wherever he went. So comfortable did he get with his fever that any time I mentioned a treatment for his condition, he got annoyed. "It won't be me, in that case," he would say. "It will change me. I will die." He denied any cure that came his way, even the possibility of it. He would get angry if one thought that there was something wrong with it. Eventually, he lived with that condition, got seriously ill and succumbed to the fever.

'Do you understand why it happened? It happened because he identified only with his body, and its condition. If there was something wrong with it, he identified with that too. Identifying only with a physical form can bring misery—you can see it, but he cannot. The modern man, on the other hand, only identifies with his brain and what goes on inside it. That brings misery. His thoughts, his emotions, his dreams and ambitions—he believes all this is his true nature. If you challenge his thoughts or emotions, he sees it as an attack on himself. He does not acknowledge it if any true self exists outside of these states. So, when you tell him to not get too attached to thoughts, he gets defensive, assuming that it will shatter his identity. He just cannot wrap his head around the fact that he can exist without his fictitious stories. He behaves like "the man with a fever", and that is his tragedy.'

'There is more to us, surely, than our thoughts and ideas,' I say. 'I mean, if I have thoughts, it clearly means that there has to be an I which is different from thoughts. Isn't it?'

'You are saying that now,' he says with a smile. He continues to smile for a long time before he continues. 'You too fell for it when emotions took over, didn't you? This happens with most people, most of the time. It's a modern curse. Most people live in their thoughts, their heads, and hardly ever get out. Inside the head, they are held hostage by their emotions. When you ask them what will they do, they say they will follow their passion. When you question their passion, they resort to instincts. The more they insist on reason, the more they are lured into a false sense of happiness.

That is the problem. There is no respite from emotions. It's a rollercoaster ride; one moment we go up, the next moment, down. You must have seen a lot of emotional struggle around. The highly evolved human mind is not at peace—it doesn't know how and when to rest. It is suffering. More and more people coming closer and yet living apart—that is the world today. There is no one to share. We have built modernity at the cost of our spirit.'

'How can we make this better?' I ask.

'Only awakened souls can bring awakening in the world. So, yes, it is theoretically possible. The only small matter is awakening yourself. An awakened soul will awaken more souls. This awakening will find itself and spread its light. Work on yourself. On your body, mind and soul—that's the trinity you need to work on.'

'I wish there was a way . . . wait, Adi, what are you doing?'

'I am not doing anything,' he says and turns to the rock next to him.

'This . . .' I point at the spider web which he is trying to unravel with his hand. So many particles, flies and moths are stuck in it.

'This,' he pauses, 'is the modern mind. Delicate. Chaotic. Attracting and catching all sorts of things.' He brings my attention to it. 'More thoughts coming in with more information. They cannot really take it, process it, but how does that matter? They are addicted.'

'Is it wrong?'

'Tell me, would it help the web if it is overladen with more particles?'

I shake my head to indicate no.

'It would not. Nor would it help the spider and its eggs that are in there. The web is the spider's tool with which it works out its life. Imagine if the web starts manipulating the spider with its strings, as though it were a puppet. What would happen to the spider, in that case? Modern minds have become like this web. They carry a lot of burden. The burden, which people proudly announce as information, knowledge and what not, causes emotional turbulence. When they experience this turbulence, they add more burden and get overwhelmed with emotions. The emotions don't stop. They keep amassing like water in a dam. If there is no check, the dam might crumble due to the overload. The same happens in your mind when you keep stress-testing the barrier.'

'Definitely not a good idea, I agree.'

'If you don't challenge your mind, it may not grow—and that's a problem. But if you burden the mind with all kinds of unhealthy things, it is an even bigger problem. Think about food. You certainly need it, but you can only digest so much of it. Beyond that, you might get a bad stomach. The modern man has the same issue in his mind. He cannot process his thoughts, cannot understand his emotions. He says a lot, but means little. He thinks a lot, but acts little.'

I do not say a word and think about all the people I have known. It feels like everyone is going through similar problems. We are suffering, not from scarcity, but abundance.

I look at Adi as silence prevails. When he is here, it feels like he, and only he, is present. Everything else fades into the background, never coming to light. I try to focus on the rock behind him, but it refuses to come forward. He alone prevails, in the fading light of this evening.

'I was waiting for you,' I say, at last. Something in me tells me that I cannot hold back any longer. He reads my mind, anyway. 'When you didn't show up, I was concerned. I was worried if you were all right.'

He looks at me and smiles. It is not often that he smiles, so every time he does, I cannot help but smile back.

'I know that too,' he says softly, after a few moments of silence.

'Then you would probably know this as well,' I say. 'I almost started to pray. Do you believe in it; praying, I mean?'

'I think prayers are often misunderstood. When people pray, they think they have got a hotline to God, and mostly, all they do is ask for favours. That's why some people, who call themselves rational, don't pray at all, while others pray blindly, without understanding the essence of a prayer.'

'Does that work? Praying the way we generally do?'

'You tell me that. Look at the world around you. Just look at it and observe its flow. This world works within the laws of nature. Have you ever seen this law breaking because of prayers? If you plant an orange tree, can you grow a mango out of it with prayers? If you are falling from the sky, the force of the earth will attract you, and no prayer will save you. Or could it?'

'I don't think so,' I shrugged.

'It won't. That's the point. No amount of requests can change the laws of nature. It's unlikely to have a divine intervention. If the creator himself intervenes, even if he does it once, the whole system could break down. People know this very well when it comes to physical conditions – they don't usually pray when they are bleeding. However, the moment it comes to the mind, they think that their problems will be solved by praying without taking any action.'

'Hmm.'

'But . . . don't forget, if done correctly, prayers can be much more than asking for favours. A prayer is a form of meditation. When you sit and close your eyes and meditate, you lose all your false sense of ego and surrender to the grandeur of this universe. In that sense, they always work. If you are asking for favours, that could be more of a hit and miss.'

'Mine did work, eventually,' I say, laughing. He laughs too.

'You, my friend, are a master, then.'

I do not say a word. The darkness is seeping in, which means it's time to light the fire. Once lit, we sit close to it and marvel at this ancient part of us.

'Were you upset?' Adi asks, with a hint of concern in his eyes.

'I think so,' I say. 'I mean, I felt a lot of things.'

'When you say, "I was upset", what is it that you are referring to as "I"? Is it your body?'

'Yes, my body hurt too.'

'That was a manifestation of your mental state. But was it hurt, really, to begin with?'

'No. I don't think so.'

'Then what was it that was really hurting?'

'Well,' I take some time to think. 'My mind felt the pain. My thoughts bogged me down and the hurt began to spread.'

'You are right,' he says. 'Thoughts can do that to you. They arise and snowball into something bigger, something inexplicable and your experience of them gives rise to emotions—which you sometimes enjoy, sometimes do not. All this can only affect you if you identify with them, as long as you have this false sense of I. Just look for it. Where is this I? On whose behalf am I getting hurt? When you look closely, you will find that it does not exist. What exists is pure awareness. The awareness is aware. That is all it does, in each moment. We look back at events in retrospect or sometimes in anticipation and that is when the dam begins to crumble. This false identity exists only in the past and the future, not in the present. In this moment, there is only awareness. We have all made mistakes and only some of us have learnt lessons,' he says and laughs loudly.

'So, this true I that you speak about, where is it? Is there anything beyond it?' I ask.

'If you keep looking, you are unlikely to find it. It's true for all the things that you truly value in your life. Happiness, for example. You cannot become happy; you can only be happy. Similarly, you cannot wait for me, nor should you; you can only be with me. And here I am. That is true for awareness as well. You cannot find awareness; you can only be aware. There is nothing that you need to find.'

'Wait,' I interrupt him. 'I had to be here in the cave to meet you, isn't it?'

'Who says so? You did not have to be here in the mountains either.'

'Are you telling me that I could have booked an appointment with you in the city?' I ask.

'Why not?' he says, laughing. 'Experiences are all around us. They change. You go to different places for different experiences. But the experiencer, that is you, does not change. The real you is untouched, it's eternal. The real you would have met me anyway, beyond the restrictions of time and space. We have met before and we will continue to meet again.'

As soon as he finishes the sentence, he gets up, takes one, two and three steps back . . . and disappears into the darkness. I walk outside, trying to look for him, but there is no sign. I come back and sit where I was sitting earlier. Looking at the fire and then at the spot where Adi was sitting, I feel a deep sense of faith inside. It is as if he neither came, nor left, but has been here all along. It's very comforting indeed. I decide to keep the flute that I had originally got for Adi and practice playing it every time I get the opportunity.

I reflect upon what he has just told me.

Why had I travelled to different countries, cities? I ask myself. Maybe I found something exciting in them, in new experiences or perhaps in reliving the old experiences. Alas! Back then, I did not spend enough time travelling in my own mind. The mind is a far more mysterious and fascinating place. It holds the key to our responses while experiencing the world. The new places merely bring sensory information. Just like new information in our books or computers, merely adding to our memories; it does little to nurture our mind. Now, I could see that only a well-nurtured mind can respond to experiences in a profound way. In fact, every experience, for a well-nurtured mind, is meaningful. It does not have to travel physically to a new place. It can do so without even leaving the room.

Which is precisely what I am going to do next.

I sit inside the cave. I will stay here and won't come out. I will travel. Not to the outside world; instead, I am going to travel in my mind and try to explore it as deeply as I can.

With these thoughts in mind—and they were the last ones—I close my eyes and become an observer. With eyes closed and without taking a step, I start the longest journey that one can ever take. Just like a traveller observes new landscapes, I am going to observe the depths of my mind. So, I sit and observe. I listen to the music of my breath, feel the rhythm of my body, and witness the magic of my mind at play— they all come together to lead me to the inner world.

The deeper I go, the more I discover the truth of Adi's words. He is the master. I know it now more than ever before.

The greatest learning is the learning by discovery. It fills you with joy and leaves a lasting imprint. I experience this soon. I discover that the cause of my misery is my identification with a separate self, which, in reality, perhaps does not even exist. Not that I am the first person to discover it, nor will I be the last. This is the kind of discovery that one has to make oneself. It cannot be taught or passed on. It is the awareness discovering itself—perhaps the most beautiful sight to behold.

I discover that I don't exist in isolation. It sounds impossible as we can see the clear distinction between different people, different things. I myself have believed it all my life. So have most people around me. Based on this naive view of the separate self, we have built the whole world. All institutions, cultures, societies, nations, states—from the ideas of human rights to personal desires to success stories—they all promote individualism. The word individual comes from indivisible, which means that it cannot be divided any further, and that it can exist in isolation. Can it, though? Can a human being exist separately, without its interconnectedness with the rest of the world? It's food for thought.

I look at my hand and find the impression of generations of humans imprinted on it. Then I look at the water in the container. Without this water, I would not exist. This water itself would not exist without the air, the earth, the sky. It's all connected. There is no separation, no boundaries. We are constantly engaged in this exchange process. I am becoming water, the sun and the moon—and they are becoming me. We are but one.

Then, what is this I? It's a false sense of ego. I know this now. There is just awareness, only awareness is aware every moment. The awareness is present everywhere. It does not think, remember, nor gets stuck in emotions. It is pure, and that is all there is. Suddenly, I think of Maya. I wish I could share this insight with her. Maybe, she will discover it by herself. That she does not exist, and nor do I. We all exist in this inter-being form, with awareness taking over all of us. All you've got to do is listen to the one who listens to the voices in your head.

I don't feel like leaving the cave today. The inner world is far too captivating to miss out on. This world is as vast and interesting as the rest of the universe, yet so close to us that we could explore it without having to travel in time or space. I sit and close my eyes. I am at peace.

'Awareness is the key to unravelling the pre-existing happiness within.'

When I open my eyes and look around, I find awareness in everything. I touch the ground with my hands and feel grateful for all the comfort it has given me. I look at the faces carved on rocks, admiring the beauty and the kind of effort people must have put into it. I feel their presence in their carvings. I take a sip of water and think about the journey it has made over millions of years. That, this water, and I—we both come from same thing, we are all stardust.

I have been in the pursuit of happiness for a long time. Now I have come to understand that this search was unnecessary. Our happiness depends on the state of our mind. If it knows how to appreciate the beauty around us, we are in a truly happy place.

What makes us happy, really? When you think about it, with clarity, you get to the heart of it.

Some would say, relationships; some would point at luxuries and pleasures; some would talk about their passion; some even their devotion. There can be a lot of answers, but in the end, it is our own mind. It holds the key. When the mind can find a way to be happy in difficult circumstances, it has achieved what the enlightened souls have achieved in the past. It might take time, it might require a lot of effort, but once achieved, it leads you to a perpetual state of contentment. There is nothing more. That is all that there is. If you can work on your mind, the rest of the world does not make much of a difference. You would still want to make it a better place, but then, you would do so without getting affected by its drama, without suffering.

I see the rocks around and think of the walls in my bedroom, back at home . . . I used to think that I know my house perfectly well. It never occurred to me that I could find anything new there. So I ventured out, hoping to discover something new elsewhere. It was my ignorance, though. It is just that I did not see it with fresh eyes, otherwise, I would have discovered countless new things every day. Not that my mind was not looking at the world around me, but it was just not looking at itself. The journey inside is quite literally mind-blowing.

The rains continue outside and so does my journey inside.

Chapter 6

The End Is the Beginning

The rains have receded, slowly and gradually and gone back to where they come from—somewhere far, far away.

The earth is damp, bathed in a musky scent; it is letting go of one season and embracing another. Ageing leaves keep falling as the days go by, merging in the same soil they grew out of and then coming back to life again. It's almost as though they never take birth or die, but simply change forms.

There has not been much to eat in the last few days; no fruits, no nuts, no berries, nothing. I start thinking like my fellow humans—consuming nature, one step at a time, and then waltzing into scarcity. On a brighter note, however, water has been aplenty. Wherever I turn, there is water. It may not taste as rich as it used to during spring and I may not feel as thirsty as I did in the summer, but water is water and it is always full of life. What about food? What do I eat? Like humanity, I am left with no choice but to depend on the next layer of nature. It has been a long time since I last hunted in the forest.

After placing a caveman trap in the forest, I come back and spend the day waiting for it to get over. When you wait, time seems to slow down—and it slows further the more impatient you get. So, it is slowing for me. *Is it even moving?* I ask myself. Without a watch, it is not easy to tell the flow of time, but perhaps it is only without a watch that you understand its true meaning. That it is a fabric woven into space, through which we travel. This is where time exists, the wisest teacher of them all. What exists in our minds is not time, but routines, schedules and deadlines.

After what seems like ages, finally the evening arrives and I go back to the forest. I walk slowly and carefully. As I approach the spot, I see a poor little thing, with its leg stuck under the rock. Is it a rabbit? Oh, yes. It appears to be in pain as I can hear it squeal. I hurry towards it—it's ironic that I am concerned about the same creature that I am supposed to consume. But, we live a life full of contradictions, don't we? Now, I lift the rock and grab the rabbit. It is still shivering and squealing; the leg has suffered the brunt of the damage. I take one final look at it and think about tonight's plan. Finally, I have it in my hand—my first substantial meal this week.

As I turn back and start to walk—savouring the roasted rabbit in my head—my foot slips on wet leaves and . . . while struggling to hold on to a bush, I fall over. Crash! A loud thud in an otherwise quiet forest! The rabbit flies in the air and descends at a quicker pace; here comes another thud! I gasp. My body feels numb, especially my head, which gets dizzy. With a laboured effort, as I try to move, I feel a stinging pain in my foot. 'Oh no! I hope I haven't broken it,' I think, still lying on my chest.

'Karma, you could have erred once, at least,' I sigh in pain and fist the ground. 'It's not fair.'

What follows next, though, takes me by surprise. The rabbit, somehow managing to crawl, moves towards me and stops next to my face.

Is it time for revenge?

No, it is not. With its large, unblinking eyes, it looks at me. It looks at me in the same way as the owl had looked at me in the forest the other night. Who are you? I try to ask but fail. I forget what has just transpired and get spellbound by its eyes. It is like a mirror, as if I am looking at my own eyes . . . Is it any different from me? Or is it my own awareness manifesting itself everywhere, creating these illusions? I put my hand on the rabbit and pet it. It does not move away; rather surprisingly, it exhibits no sign of fear.

'Don't worry. You are safe,' I say.

The rabbit listens with its ears adjusting and pointing like antennae. Then it moves closer—a stamp of acknowledgement, perhaps. We lie on wet leaves for quite some time; both injured, both unsure of what to do. The dinner plans are spoiled for both of us, but at least I am not going to have trust issues with food.

'I am sorry, dear rabbit,' I say.

Seeing the forest turn dark, I muster the strength to move my body. The pain is excruciating. I drag myself and somehow manage to stand on my feet. I pick up the rabbit too. I don't know why, but to my heart, the separation did not seem right after all we have been through in this short time. The rabbit is responding; it does not fear me, or the wilderness around, and sits comfortably in my hands. It is soft and warm. In the wild, you come across things or creatures that no man has ever laid his finger on. You can see beauty in its purest form, untouched, unspoiled. This rabbit, on the other hand, has lost those credentials.

Now, we head towards the cave. Thankfully, nothing is broken. It's a slow walk; my right foot stings with every step I take. The darkness does not help either, especially when you are treading slippery slopes. The rabbit is in pain too, but it seems curious to see the world from a new perspective, perhaps enjoying its first-ever flight. Or perhaps, it is watching suspiciously to check if I have got more tricks up my sleeve. However, for me, the plans have changed.

As I look at it, I feel I was going to make a mistake by taking its life. They were my instincts, or were they? Did I grow up with them? Sometimes, it is hard to tell whether it's a natural instinct or outside influences. Back in the city, I did not give too much thought to such matters. I did not have too much time, anyway. Here, in the wild, when I do have time, I really feel bad about what I did to the poor rabbit. Love comes naturally; it does not require any reason, unlike hate, which requires a lot of explanation.

It makes me think about my father, who would take me to the butcher's shop and ask me to see him work.

'Death should always be personal,' he would say. 'It cannot just be a story you read in the news or a fact you overlook.' His words make so much sense now. We simply think of death as a fact, as a number, especially when it comes to animals. But when it comes to an animal that we have known or built a close relationship with, we develop a different emotion. We may still kill animals for our survival, but then, it would be a very different experience than seeing it merely as a number. That death would be personal, as my father would put it.

Upon reaching the cave, I take a few deep breaths and rest for a while. It is cold. The cave must have waited for me with the anticipation of food. But, tonight is going to be another night of deprivation. *That's fine*, I tell myself, *at least I have company*. Isn't that something? At least one of us won't be hungry, as there is plenty of grass outside the cave. I place the rabbit in the cave and bring some grass for it. It hesitates at first, but then chews on it. How easily this little creature has put its trust in me—it surprises me. There is an advantage in not being able to think too much. It's the thoughts that bring most of our suffering, as Adi had told me.

I arrange a handful of dry leaves, some twigs and sticks, and light a fire. Keeping an eye on the rabbit and making sure that it does not feel threatened, I add more fuel, making a small contribution to global warming. The rabbit looks on, with nervousness and curiosity, but at no point does it make any movement. 'You will get comfortable with this,' I say. 'This warmth is addictive.' It looks at the fire and then at me, its eyes glowing red. As the glancing goes on, eventually, our eyes cross each other. Neither turns our gaze away. Time stops. I find a strange sense of awe in those red, sparkling eyes. Maybe, it does too. What a sight it is! Two species, connected through millions of years of evolution, looking at each other, recognizing their lost past. Trust comes naturally between two life forms, especially in the wild.

In the next few days, the two of us spend more time together. It's the beginning of my friendship with Bilbo. Yes, Bilbo—that's the name I came up with. It was a fairly obvious choice, given its hobbit-like ears and hair, and how it sniffs. Bilbo, I soon discover, is a playful bunny. He rarely sits still and hops around in excitement almost all the time. When I light a fire in the evening, he jumps to the other side and stares at me from a distance. I like this feeling. It is as if we don't really exist until someone is there to observe us. When Bilbo is away—rolling in grass or hiding behind rocks—I feel my heart skipping a beat. 'Where have you gone? Come back, Bilbo,' I say out loud, hoping that he would understand my words, or at least get the gist of them. In a matter of a few days, he has begun to understand me. What an incredible creature! The more time we spend together, the more attached I get. It is just not me. Bilbo feels the same, I think, as he starts chasing me as soon as he sees me getting out of sight.

This has got me thinking. I feel like being at home, once again. Attachment, in a really strange way, is bogging me down. How can I create that balance? I ponder over this as I gaze into the mesmerizing fire. Caveman TV! I say it out loud to Bilbo and laugh.

Maybe, attachment is not right. It brings pain, causes anxiety. I know the problem, but sadly, the problem and solution only exist inside my head. When it comes to action, I feel helpless. We are creatures of emotion, after all, and that does not help very much. Sometimes we get so blindsided by our emotions that we confuse attachment for love. Love does not crush you under its weight; it elevates you, makes you fly. In its purest form, love is liberating. I remind myself of my purpose. Why am I here in the wild, in the first place? Why am I away from the crowds? I know why. To get rid of my shackles of attachment and experience freedom in its entirety. To find love in its purest form, not in the selfish form where I am more concerned about taking rather than giving. Love should be about the act of loving; it's a verb, not a noun. Otherwise, it becomes mere consumption, and hence, an addiction.

Now that I look at Bilbo, I feel trapped in conflicting emotions. A part of me wants to hold on to him and a part of me wants to let go. The first instinct appears more powerful, and is having its way, which is what it does most of the time. How do I tame it? What if I don't? Is suffering inevitable every time there is attachment? For the time being, I keep all these questions aside and start playing with Bilbo. My struggle with emotions and playfulness goes on.

Today, for whatever reason (more likely, there is a reason and I don't see it), Bilbo is in a different mood. Ever since the morning has arrived, he is trying to get away from me. The more I try to catch him, the farther he runs away. And the more he runs away, the more I chase him. Does he want me to chase him? Does he want to disappear? This hide and seek has gone on in and around the cave, and now, under the sunshine, we have reached the edge of the forest. This time, he runs not on the stone path but through the bushes. I run in that direction. After a long chase, I see him hastening deep into the woods. I follow him and keep running until I run out of breath. I sit down at one point.

I sigh in despair as I look down. It was long coming. Somewhere in my heart, I knew this. Perhaps the time has come to accept. How long will I keep shying away from reality? How long will I live in denial? I think of Adi and all that he has told me, and say to myself, *Just let go*. I know that we have shared good memories, forged a special bond, but this is it, my dear friend. Now is the time. Holding on can't be good. I can see that, at least a part of me does, but Bilbo can't. It is my responsibility. So, I decide not to chase him any more. Instead, I tell myself to come to terms with it. 'This is the end . . . my only friend . . . the end . . .' I hum along; not of everything, but of one of the many journeys we would embark upon.

I look around. The vivid colours fill me with a myriad of emotions. I can see sheep at a distance. Hang on . . . are those people? *Hardly any difference*, I tell myself and laugh. They seem stationary; however, the clouds behind them drift slowly. What a soothing sight! And then . . . transgressing suddenly, out of nowhere, I hear a sobbing sound. Who is it? I turn around and take a few steps towards the sound. It's *him*.

'Shakti . . .' I say. 'What happened? Are you all right?'

He looks at me and does not respond. I move closer to him and put my arm around his shoulders.

'What happened, Shakti?' I ask him.

'Ganga, my wife . . . she left us,' he says and cries in pain. The sound of a cry comes from many places, but the most painful ones come straight from the gut; it was one such cry. He is inconsolable.

I am shocked. I don't know what to say. I hug him and sit there in silence. Sometimes words are not enough. Sometimes they are not even required.

'She fell off the roof,' he goes on. 'She injured her head. The bleeding was severe. She had lost too much blood before we could do anything. We could do nothing, Jeet.'

'Wasn't there any doctor nearby?' I ask naively. It's just that I cannot accept what Shakti has told me. My mind is unable to accept Ganga's death and is looking for possibilities that could have avoided this.

'The clinic is many miles away. There is no road here, no cars. We carried her ourselves, and . . . and she stopped breathing on the way,' he says and wipes his tears. 'I still took her to the clinic. I was hoping that something will change her fate. But who can change it? The doctor said that he could not do anything. It was too late.'

'I am so sorry,' I sigh. Tears roll down my cheeks too. I feel deeply connected with Shakti in this moment.

'Come with me to my house,' he says at last. 'The kids like you. They will feel better in your company.'

'Of course,' I say. 'It would mean the world to me if I could be of any help to you and your family.'

We walk towards the village. Along the way, Shakti gathers and moves the livestock, despite his obvious struggles. He seems to be lost, unable to focus. We walk listlessly; yet, he keeps stumbling every few steps. Now, I hold him by one hand, and tend to the livestock with a stick in the other. Even the animals look sad. They are reluctantly walking without making any sound.

We reach the village around dusk. Shakti washes his hands in a stream in the fading light. He searches carefully for a reflection in the water, as if it's not him but someone else he is seeking. I can see it. He is still searching for *her*, hoping to find a sign. When he catches me looking at him, he stretches his lips to present a smile—his eyes are still soaked in pain.

The house feels colder than the last time I was here. The air reeks of gloominess. Only silence prevails. Every other sound, coming from outside the house, is heard distinctly. I can see that the balance of the family has been disturbed as an important constituent of it is missing. I think of Ganga's smile, still being reflected inside these four walls. I suspect Shakti sees it too, and that's why he is peering at everything.

Amma is sitting where she was sitting the last time. Has she even moved? She looks at me and—with what seems like a tremendous effort on her part—she smiles uncomfortably but finds it difficult to hold back her tears.

'Where are you, my children?' she says in a loud voice, but even that does not travel very far. 'Look who is here.' She tries again.

'Mehak hasn't left the room ever since Ganga passed away,' Amma tells me. 'I cannot force her,' she adds. I nod in agreement. Aakash has been asking to see his mother. 'Either bring her here, or take me to her,' he demands adamantly. No one quite knows how to explain the concept of death to a three-year-old. And no one knows how to tell him that neither of his demands could be fulfilled. Amma asks me if I could do that. 'There must be some way,' she says and expects me to respond. I don't exactly know how to answer, so I nod again.

I go to bed, with only one thought in my mind: death. It's a subject that we neither address nor ignore; it is constantly on the sidelines. When we turn a blind eye to it, it haunts us; and when we tend to it, there seems no way to make sense of it. But it is always around, lurking in the shadows.

When death strikes somewhere close, on someone we know or care about, we can't help but think about the impermanence of life. Then, swayed by the passage of time, we forget about it. When death is in the news, we usually turn to other topics. Remembering and forgetting is the game we play with death. More importantly, rarely do we face the crude reality of our own death. That one day we won't be alive as we are today. That the world would continue to exist after us, as it has been existing before us. Death is something that always happens to other people—while we glance at it from a distance. After all, we have not seen ourselves die, have we? What would that feel like? All these thoughts overwhelm me and I start sweating profusely. I get up from the bed and fold my hands and look up to the heavens.

The idea of death has been lurking in the shadows of my mind, but it has never knocked on the doors of my awareness in the same way as it does now. Now that it has, I don't know how to open the door and face it. I try to resist, but to no effect. I tremble. What will happen after death? What if I die tomorrow? What should I do? It's a frightening thought.

A thought travels through the great expanse and finds me. It's that of Adi. His presence, his words, and all the things he has taught—they all seem to appear in a flash. That's the power of thoughts. They can transcend the limitations of physical boundaries and find us. I close my eyes and meditate upon the idea of death. For that, I have to begin with life. What is life? I try to find it inside. The search continues as I lay down on my back and stare at the ceiling. Soon, my eyes shut their windows, and I experience a deeply relaxing, restful state, without really falling asleep. It's a blissful state. It takes all my fears away. The thought of death disappears and the so-called reality begins to pervade. I can see myself flowing through time and space, with birth and death merely two stations among countless others on this journey.

When the sun comes up in the morning, the house remains as quiet as it was when the sun went down. The children do not play, nor do they make any sound. I sit beside Amma as we sip on the morning tea. She seems to be much more active than the last time I had seen her. She is managing the kitchen all by herself. I insisted on making tea, but she would not let me. Despite being old, she has been able to understand and take on new challenges. Perhaps that helps her in dealing with the pain.

Shortly afterwards, I go to the shed where Shakti is sitting with the cattle and I sit next to him.

'I can't imagine the pain you are going through,' I say. 'Be strong. I hope you find peace today.'

'I hope so too,' he shakes his head and looks at the cattle. He is still not able to maintain eye contact. 'I don't know how to live without her. A voice in my head asks, where is she?'

'She is in your heart,' I say. 'This is where she has been all along. Earlier, she was also there, physically. Now, what remains is her essence. That is the reason she might be a lot closer to you than you would think.'

'Actually . . . what you are saying, it makes sense. I have felt it too. Strangely, I feel now I know her better. When she was here, I never really sat and thought about her. Now that she is gone, it's all I do, and I love her even more.'

'The physical body changes its form throughout our lives, but the essence of a person, that which you feel about Ganga now—that remains. That is her true nature . . . and no one can take that away from you.'

'But . . .' he mumbles, 'it still bothers me. So many regrets. All that could have been, all that could go differently. I keep thinking about that final moment.'

'You know, after coming here, I realized how thinking about death could be liberating. Especially when we look at it in the right context.'

'What do you mean?'

'Death, in its different forms, is all around us. It takes place all the time, inside us, outside us. Whatever we do, it has a starting and an end. This day, our meeting, seasons, months and years—they will end, or die, if we use that word. Transitions contain both birth and death. The death of something, leading to the birth of something else. This transition, when we experience it, causes great pain and discomfort. It's a reminder of our separation from the heavens. This separation—along with the pain—is reflected in every separation that we experience. When a meeting with a beloved ends, it pains us; when our child leaves home, that pains us too. Separation is painful. That is why we resist it. We don't like this change even if there is some good in store for us. Attachments become our shackles. We don't feel like leaving our old house even when we know that we are moving to a better house. Birth and death are like that. But then, they are just two events on this journey.'

'What do you think, then? What does death do to a person?'

'I don't know all there is to be known. But I can tell based on what I have learnt in the last few days about death. We take births and we die. If we are taking birth that means we were there before the birth. Anything that takes birth has to die. And anything that dies has to take birth again. So, there is a self, beyond the cycles of life and death. That is the self we should seek and experience. We are life, captured in our bodies. Like water captured in a drop. The drop may lose its shape or form, but the water remains—in one form or another.'

'This is not the end, you mean?'

'A great poet once said, "Ends and beginnings—there are no such things; there are only middles."'

'Hmm . . .'

'I understand that you are in pain. But don't you think it will be good for her, wherever she is, if you lead a good life and look after the children well?'

'I suppose, but it is not easy to overcome this pain. Or even accept this.'

'You are right. Accepting the reality of living life without your loved one is a challenge, full of pain. However, this is a necessary first step that you must take.'

'You know,' Shakti says and looks into my eyes for the first time today. 'I had a dream last night. Ganga was there. She was calling for help. I was trying to reach out to her with my hands but she kept falling and I could not hold on to her. When I woke up, I realized that she was gone.'

'Dreams can reveal so much,' I say. 'If you think about it, this life is also like a dream. It just goes by in the blink of an eye. It is just a matter of time. We are all in line. But then, that does not mean that the dream will get over and there will be nothing. After the dream, there will be new reality.'

'Yes,' he says and folds his hands. 'I just pray for her wherever she is.'

I fold my hands too, as we pray together.

'Then what did you do once the dream was over?' I ask.

'Nothing. I went to sleep again. Albeit, with some difficulty; but in the end, it was somewhat peaceful.'

'She too is at peace now,' I say.

Shakti nods. 'I hope so,' he says. 'That is all I want. All she has done in this life was look after everyone. She deserves to be in a good place. And what did she get in return? Death.'

'Death is not something that we should look down upon. It is a reality that we must face. If you think about it, you will find many answers. In fact, the meditation upon death itself is a healing practice.'

'How do you do that?'

'You remember the one you have lost. However, you remember them not in the sense that you want to possess them. No, that is selfish. You remember them selflessly. You remember them as an expression of love. Because once their physical body has merged with nature, your love, your remembrance is the form they exist in. You remind yourself of that love every single time you miss them. You find them within you. When you do that, you can build a much closer relationship with them by acknowledging that they no longer physically remain in your life.

'At the same time, recognizing the certainty and unpredictability of death is important. The fact that we can die any time, in any place, is a reality we must embrace and prepare ourselves for. Work on creating a greater awareness. How your body is changing. How your mind is changing. Pay close attention to it. Then slowly, you will see that there is a self beyond your body and mind, and that self transcends the cycle of birth and death. We come from this universe and go back to it. Never created, never destroyed, the true self will always stay. So will Ganga's true self.'

'That is a fear I have. What would happen to my children after I die?'

'That is why it is good to reflect upon death. Our anxieties about death are perfectly reasonable and we must address them.'

He nods. 'Could you do something for me?' he asks. 'Can you talk to Mehak? More than myself, I worry about her.'

'I will,' I say. 'Don't you worry.'

I go inside and knock on the door. 'Is anybody in there?' I ask. Mehak is inside, but she doesn't respond. 'I am coming in, okay?' I open the door and enter. She is sitting on the ground, wiping her tears. I try to talk to her but she keeps ignoring my presence.

'You know, Mehak,' I say, 'your mother is right here with you.'

This time, she looks at me. She does not say a word and keeps looking at me intently. Shakti has followed me and is standing behind the door.

'Look at your hands. Aren't they exactly like your mother's? And not just hands, go and look at your face in the mirror. You would see that her hands, her face is growing within you. This is what happens when our parents leave us. They become a part of us. We are not separate, but a reflection of them. Our parents don't take rebirth elsewhere, they take it within us. Just go there and look in the mirror.'

She gets up and hurries towards a box. After opening the box, she takes out a small, round mirror and looks in it. She also looks at her hands and touches one with the other. 'Mother,' she says and begins to cry.

'Say this to your mother with me.'

She waits for me to continue.

'Mother, I know that you are there . . . I am here, continuing this life for you . . . I am breathing for you . . . I am looking through your eyes, walking on your feet . . . I am enjoying my life with you . . . You are living this life through me, by becoming a part of me . . .'

She repeats every sentence after me. Although the tears continue to roll down, they also seem to bring out the pain that was hiding deep inside.

'I accept that you are in this new form.'

She repeats that too.

Suddenly, she sees her father who is standing at the door, and runs towards him.

Father and daughter hold each other and tears continue to flow. I look at them from a distance. Both are saying something and both are crying. Now, Amma and Aakash join them too. I know that they feel the pain of this loss, but I also know that their healing has begun.

Chapter 7

Perpetual Seekers

Life in the village is different. It is unlike the two places I have spent a lot of time in—the city and then the cave; two places that lie at the opposite ends of the social spectrum. One crowded and noisy, the other secluded and quiet.

However, life in the village is far more balanced. You are surrounded by people, but not too many. You have your space, but not so much that you feel lonely. There is a murmur of life around—not loud noises or a deafening silence. In fact, different shades of murmurs prevail as the day goes by. People wake up early and take to their duties. Not only people, the nonhuman residents of the village do that too. The latter coo and caw, and moo and mew, and ramble here and there. The former also do the same but they believe they are different. *Talking and walking* is the expression they use for their own coos and moos and rambles.

Looking at the morning sky, with new colours appearing and disappearing on the horizon, I do some calculations in my head. Which month is it? Time is whizzing by; more months have gone by than there are to come. The sun seems to be getting lazy and has been delaying its arrival with each passing day, and yet, the rooster is always on time (when it comes to its crowing). One, two, three . . . and there it goes—*kuk-a-doo-koo*—announcing that the path is clear of predators. There are not many predators in reality, but such is the habit of the rooster that it cannot let go. It is not different from people in this regard; we create our habits and then the habits start defining and dictating our identities.

There it goes again, with its kuk-a-doo-koo. It wakes me up in the same way every morning. If the rooster were a man, I am certain that it would soon get bored of its job. The hard-working rooster goes on with its warnings, day after day, until it goes the way of the dinosaurs, its evolutionary ancestors.

This particular morning feels disagreeably colder than the previous one or the one before that. Although I have been having this feeling every day ever since I came here. I curl up in front of the fire and gulp a cup of tea as soon as I get out of bed. The warmth creates a tingling sensation in my quivering body. The world outside seems to be shrinking too, at this time of the year. The streams have grown fewer in numbers, some even disappeared. The air has dried and so has the fragrance it carries. When the sun comes up, it warms me up. It's a sweet feeling. When it goes down, it makes me wait for the next day when it will show up again. That same hope makes the whole world live in peace and plan for tomorrow. As far as I am concerned, I have no plans. Today is what I have and it is where I wish to be. I sigh, and a misty cloud comes out of my mouth.

Shakti, along with the kids, left for a pilgrimage earlier this morning. It will take them two days to get there and another two to return. They will stay in a village at the end of the first day and in the temple on the second. There, they will complete the remaining rituals for Ganga and offer food to the needy. That should take an entire day. It would be a source of healing, I believe. In the last few days when I stayed with the family, I have seen them learning to accept the tragedy and trying to make their way ahead. They are taking small steps, one at a time. Washing the utensils, cleaning the dust, making tea, serving others—it all helps when you are trying to row through a storm. Additional responsibilities have kept them busy, and so, they are beginning to embrace life as it comes.

Amma has stayed back, and as it happens in a village, neighbours are eager to look after her. It is in this place that the old African proverb—it takes a village to raise a child—makes sense to me. Any task, when shared, becomes enjoyable. This is what is happening today. Someone or the other has been coming in and bringing food or tea. It goes on and on and on. Due to this influx, I am getting to see faces that I have not seen before. Nor have I seen these many food items. Amma, being the kind woman that she is, passes every plate to me and says, 'Why don't you eat something? Don't say no, you have to eat and finish it.' I oblige, every time. More breads. More vegetables. More tea. More work for my digestive system too. I have not eaten this much for as long as I can remember. A burp is not too far away; I can sense it brewing in me.

I was planning to go back to the cave, but then Naru, a young man from the village, asked me to stay back. 'They are coming,' he said in a dramatic voice. 'You should meet them. I am telling you, you should meet them. You may not get another chance.' When I asked him who *they* were, he said, 'They have been coming here for god knows how long. And they will keep coming. People like me will come and go, but they will continue to visit. No wonder they are different from the rest of us.'

'But who are *they*?' I pressed again, hoping he would understand the question this time. My mistake.

'They are what they are,' he added. 'And they are not one but many, and still they seem like one. They are something else, I am telling you. You will know when you see them. You have to see them.'

I found the explanation a little bizarre. So I tried to wrap my head around it. 'Tell me, what do these people do? What are they like?'

'They come and go, but they never leave,' he said. 'Everyone is so fond of them. You will know when you see them.' That did not help and confused me further. But now I was very curious. What was going on? Who were these people that this man was talking about? I asked myself these questions and waited to see them.

'Come on, just meet them. It will change your life,' he said with an air of confidence.

I did not say a word—there was no point, anyway. But meeting these people sounded like a good idea to me.

So, I stayed.

They arrive at the time when the sun is right above our heads and the shadows have disappeared right below our toes. Suddenly, a hush descends over the crowd and everyone's gaze turns and gets fixed at the pavement. Then come the footsteps. One, and another, and another . . . It goes on for a while before I can finally see their faces. Those bright, beaming faces with smiles imprinted on them. I examine their faces, their movements as they arrive. There are seven of them: five men and two women. One of them seems to be considerably old. He walks slowly and in measured steps, ahead of his companions. They are wearing somewhat similar clothes—loose robes in plain colours, draped around their bodies. It's hard to tell from a distance who is who, except the old man. They are light on their feet, and they move as if they have just descended from the sky and are floating in the air. I look at their smiles and cannot look away. It makes me smile too. Without any conscious effort, I take a

few steps forward, trying to get closer to the visitors.
I am not alone; the villagers do the same.

Soon, the murmurs turn into conversations. These
seven seem to know everyone and everything about
everyone. How is your mother now? What happened
to the crops? When is your brother coming back?
They are talking as if they have known each other
all their lives. People embrace them and hold them.
Some smiling, some crying. The villagers can no longer
hold themselves back and start talking, all at once—
an indistinct chatter spreads in the air. From what
I hear, I can tell that they are discussing Ganga's death.
Some have folded their hands and are chanting her
name as they bow down to the heavens and pray. Then,
suddenly . . . the chatter dies down and they rush to the
other side.

'What is going on?' I ask Naru, who is holding me
by my arm in nervousness. He says something that
I could not hear. So I ask him to repeat it.

'The liberation of the soul,' he says. 'They are
preparing for the comfortable passage of Ganga's soul.
I don't think that her soul has got freedom yet. It's here.
I feel it. Many villagers have seen her in their dreams
recently. This is the need of the hour. Otherwise, you
never know about ghosts and—'

Before he could finish, I turn to the crowd.

The two ladies build a small, pyramid-like structure
of stones and leave one opening towards the north. The
other five men stand around it and bow. The villagers
stand behind them, with eyes closed and hands folded.
The chanting begins. It starts with Ganga's name and

grows into a rhythmic song. First the two women, then the five men, and then the entire village joins in—and the air reverberates with their chanting. The two women's hands move in the direction of the opening and spread outwards, into the sky. Everyone else follows.

As the chants dissolve in the air, the villagers move towards each other and start thanking their gods. 'The soul has departed to the next world,' Naru tells me. The villagers hug, first the seven visitors, and then each other. Some of them come to me and hug me. These are not quick hugs; rather, they embrace the other person fully, without saying a word. Tears roll down. Everyone's deepest pain comes out in this atmosphere. The physical embrace is such a rare thing in today's time. Sometimes we look down upon it. But here, it feels like the right thing to do; and it feels . . . beautiful.

'You should go and talk to them,' Naru urges me. The older gentleman is not far and, I suppose, he can hear Naru's words. 'They are really great people. You have no idea what they are going to gift you. I am also waiting for my gift.'

Somewhat embarrassingly, I turn towards the old man, who looks bemused.

'Hello,' I say to him. Naru looks at us, alternately, with his mouth wide open.

'Don't worry. He is always like that,' the old man says. 'Never seen anyone gossip the way he does.' Naru hears the last part and slips away quietly.

'Thank you,' I say.

'That's all right. I am sorry I did not have the time to introduce myself,' the man says. 'How are you doing?'

'I am doing well. Thank you for asking. My name is Jeet. And yours?'

'I am Paul,' he says. 'Glad to meet you, Jeet. Adi told me about you.'

'Adi . . . how do you know him?'

'Well, to be fair, who does not know him? People know him, sometimes by different names, but they know him. But . . . if you really want to hear about how I came to know him, that will take some time.'

'I have all the time in this world,' I say, smiling.

'Do you? Does anyone really have that?' he laughs. 'Come here. Why don't you sit here with me?'

'Of course,' I say and sit next to him. The sun is shining in the clear blue sky. The murmur around us goes on.

'All right,' he begins. 'I will tell you then. I have spent a lot of time with Adi in these mountains. I have known him for longer than you would think. When he first came here, a lot of people gathered to see him. Chaos broke out. There was excitement. Some considered him to be from the other world. Some called him a magician. They waited for him to show some of his tricks. They thought maybe he would create fire out of thin air or fly in the sky or vanish into the darkness. He did none of that. He simply sat there. That was that. Nothing else. Seeing him sitting there, not doing anything, people started leaving. They were underwhelmed by what they had seen or should I say, not seen. Luckily, the seven of us were also there. We were the only ones that did not leave. We saw him sitting in bliss and saw the real magic. Sitting still, day after day, was the greatest magic one could perform. We knew that. So, we stayed and waited for him to talk to us. Which took quite some time. But, in the end, it was worth it. We learnt so much from him. In fact, each one of us learnt a different lesson. That is his greatness; he can teach every student something new. That is why we keep coming here. We meet him. We spend time with him. And we go back, only to come again.'

'Back where?'

'I don't live very far. Somewhere in the mountains over there,' he points. 'But these friends of mine, they come from different places, quite far actually. That's Dobby, he comes from as far west as civilization goes. He is always learning, always acquiring new knowledge. That fellow standing over there, that's Angiras. He lives in the southern part of this country. He travels from north to south and along the way he talks to everyone he meets. He has been a source of mysticism for southerners. Those two women are over there, they are Mizar and Audrey. They come from the desert. They have been friends for a long time and have left everything behind. Both of them have been completely devoted to Adi. I think they learn more than anyone else. Tian, sitting there, comes from the far east. He lives with animals and looks after them when he goes back. And finally, Marik, he comes from the north-western coast. He is someone who understands the human body really well. He was a doctor before he came here and joined us. But he still heals people, although in a completely different way.'

'It's incredible how despite being so different, coming from different parts, you are able to work towards the same goal,' I say, unable to hide my enthusiasm. I try to repeat those names in my head. It is not going to be easy. 'Do you always travel together?' I ask.

'Here, in these mountains,' he says, 'you would see us travelling together. We come every year during this time and go to the sacred mountain. There, we pray on the full moon night. We share what happened in the past year and what we plan to do next. After that, we go back and do our work there. No communication, until the next year. No phones, no letters. We know we will come here and embark on this journey to the sacred mountain.'

'That is fascinating.'

'Life is as fascinating as we make it to be,' he says, expressing gratitude with a smile. It makes me speechless. The sun shines behind his head and I can no longer look directly at him. What is it, really? I don't know. And the fact that I don't know what it is, fills me with the insatiable appetite to know more.

'Would you like to join us for a meal?' he asks.

'I would join you, surely,' I say. 'I may not able to eat but that's another matter.'

He laughs. 'I know. These lovely people . . . they have a peculiar way of showering you with affection—they fill you with food.' He turns to the other side and says, 'Come, Marik. Meet Jeet.'

We exchange greetings and sit next to each other.

'Why don't you eat, Jeet?' Marik asks me.

'I feel so stuffed. I lost count of how much I have eaten since the morning. Could you suggest something for that, doctor?'

'You should not have eaten that much,' he says, very matter-of-factly.

'It is all right once in a while, isn't it?' I ask him.

He stays quiet and smiles. I know he disagrees, but he doesn't say a word. He remains silent for some time. Perhaps he is avoiding even the possibility of a conflict. Silence. That is all he offers. It sounds easy but it is one of the toughest things to do. Especially in a world which repeatedly reminds us that we should disagree and hold our ground. That it is good for our careers and what not. But here, outside the world of occupational jargon, all of that seems to make no sense.

'Isn't . . .' I want to say something, but then I hold back immediately and ask myself, *What is it in me that wants to disagree? Is it my ego that is not giving an inch? Because at the fundamental level, there is no difference between us. And there is no disagreement either.* It helps me go through this moment of turbulence. It comforts me. The conflict between two people is like burning a bridge. Just like love between two people is like building one, full of happiness.

They continue to eat, slowly and mindfully. Sitting there, I notice a dog meekly approaching the food items. It looks almost ashamed of itself, but its hunger is such that shame has no say. Audrey, upon seeing it, offers it some bread. The dog devours the bread in no time and then starts looking at her again. It is still hungry, drooling. Now, she is left with only one piece of bread. Difficult choice? Apparently not, for her. Without a second thought, she gives it to the dog. She might be hungry, but the relief on her face is something else. Such is the joy of giving.

'Can I ask you something, Audrey?' I say.

'Yes, please,' she responds.

'If you remain hungry and keep feeding others, isn't it like depriving a creature, that is you, of food?'

She smiles. 'That is a common concern,' she says. 'But if you follow this thought, like most other thoughts, it takes us to fear. Most of our actions are driven by fear. It dictates that if we do not look after ourselves, something terrible will happen. Someone will grab our land or steal our jobs. It's only our fear. One thing that we should remember is, we are not separate from our surroundings. In an ailing world, it's only a matter of time before humanity would succumb. The health of the earth, water and air decides the fate of the beings here.'

'I understand. Everything depends on everything else. We do not and cannot exist in separation. The underlying reality is that of oneness.'

'I would say,' now Tian joins us, 'even if we believe that we exist in isolation, we should still ask ourselves this question. That how can our appetite be more important than a poor animal's suffering?'

'You are right,' Audrey says.

I nod in agreement. Tian pats the dog and starts playing with it. The dog jumps around in excitement. When we treat animals with love and care, they return all of it and more.

'Hey,' Paul taps me on my shoulder. I turn around immediately.

'Hey, Paul!'

'We will be leaving for the sacred mountain shortly,' he informs me. 'Would you like to join us?'

'Absolutely! I would love to,' I say. 'It is not too far, is it?'

'Well, if I can get there, surely you can too,' he laughs.

I want to say that was not what I had meant, but it feels unnecessary. Back in the day, I would argue over the smallest of things. In fact, it was one of my favourite pastimes. If someone erred in grammar, I would chase them with words and sentence them for anti-semantic behaviour. Not any more, though.

We start to walk. The villagers bid us goodbye and send their good wishes with us to the mountain. The path is a different one than what I take for the cave. It goes straight to the sacred mountain in the east. The terrain is narrow and steep and if one does not walk carefully, he might risk falling off the edge. We have formed a straight line; everyone follows the footsteps of the person in front. The climb gets steeper as we go higher and get tired quickly. That means, the breaks are frequent. When we decide to take a break, we sit down and share stories. I listen more than I speak. And that is a good idea, considering the company that

I have. After all, there must be a reason why we have two ears but only one mouth, I remind myself.

'You know so much about body, mind and spirit,' I say when I hear them speak on the subject. 'I could tell that based on the conversation that we are having. How is that?'

'Perhaps you don't know, Jeet,' Paul tells me, 'the seven of us, when we go back, we share our stories and experiences with people. Since we share these things often, we too learn a few things here and there.'

'I am not surprised. Given the kind of knowledge you have, I would expect no less.'

'Thank you,' he smiles and bows his head gently. 'All thanks to Adi. He taught us all this and he asked us to share this knowledge.'

'That is very thoughtful of him, and of course, you deserve all the credit. I mean, everyone, everywhere is getting access to this wisdom.'

'Indeed,' he says. 'But, I think these six deserve more credit than I do. I stay in these mountains and speak to people who understand our language. So, for me, it is not challenging to share. These people, on the other hand, have done an admirable job. They have to climb higher mountains when they go back. They have to work in a different culture, speak to people who have very different perspectives on everything. That is the real test.'

'True,' I exclaim. 'I wonder, how they do that?'

'That is the real question . . . and the answer is even more interesting. Initially, there was a lot of hesitation in people's minds. They would resist everything that was foreign to them. So, when my friends acquired wisdom from Adi, they translated it into the practices that were already a part of their respective cultures. They wrapped this new knowledge in the existing stories of their culture and shared it with people. When you share ancient, foreign wisdom in this form, people do not resist; on the contrary, they welcome it.'

'I can only appreciate what all of you are doing.'

He smiles and says, 'Time for us to get moving.' And so, we do.

I keep listening and observing along the way. These people do not plan, nor do they seem to worry about obstacles. When I ask them if they have considered the risk of wild animals, they say that one must look beyond fear and treat the wild creatures with compassion. I look at them in awe. There is nothing extraordinary, but there are all the ingredients of simple ordinariness which is no less fascinating. It is like watching a plant grow into a tree and bear fruits. It's ordinary, but it's beautiful. Freedom brings completeness to humans. It is essential to our nature. A nurtured mind is a way to a nurtured soul.

Finally, we reach the top of the mountain. I heave a deep sigh on seeing the spectacular view. The sun has just set and darkness has not yet arrived. The twilight period is oddly comforting and not just to the eyes. I spread my arms as I embrace the fading sky and immediately feel a deep sense of being at peace. When I turn around, everyone else is doing it too. It's beautiful.

As darkness seeps in, we light a fire that warms us from the inside out. There is something about it, the fire, the sparks that float away towards the stars, Caveman TV at its very best. We sit with another human being around the fire and we cannot hold back. The stories just begin to flow. They all share, one by one, about their experiences over the last year. Then, they turn towards me.

'Adi told us a lot of things about you,' Paul says. The others nod along.

'Really?' I act surprised.

'Yes.'

'What did he tell you?' I ask curiously. It always makes me wonder what Adi thinks of me, and here I am, wondering again.

'Well, there were a lot of things,' he says softly. 'But those are for some other time. The most important thing he said was that you are a seeker and someone who seeks eventually finds the way. He might get late, but he will arrive. What is important is that we continue on our unending quest to find that connection between our world and the other.'

'Hmm,' I take time to absorb his words.

'He said he would be away for a while.'

'Is that so?' I wonder where he has gone this time. Would he come back? I don't know. 'You know, he never told me about you. I don't understand that part.'

'Ha ha. Maybe he wanted to keep us a secret.' Now, everyone laughs too.

'Or maybe he wanted you to meet me and share your secrets.'

'Maybe. In that case . . . nothing is the secret.'

'Nothing?'

'Yes. Nothingness is the secret, if there was any. Nothing is the essence of everything. From nothing comes something and pervades us to make everything. If we had kept something with us, it would have been very difficult to carry. Something is heavy. It becomes hard to play with. But when you have nothing, you are open to limitless possibilities. You can be anything. You can do anything. That is what we are—nothing.'

'That is a rare feat to achieve. But how does one live their life in nothingness?'

'One lives without fears, without expectations. All one has, when one has nothing, is gratitude. That is a good place to start a life.'

'What do you do with your memories, your thoughts?'

'They are where they are, in our brains. That is where they should be. Just like our blood is in the body, flowing constantly, these neurons fire constantly. We do not worry about blood. It is moving on its own. In the same way, we should not worry about our thoughts. Let them do their job, and we do ours.'

'Interesting. You know what I have learnt after spending time with you? I figured that what I considered a radical way of living is not really that radical. On the contrary, it's an ordinary life, if I may call it that. What we call ordinary life, back in the city, is not really ordinary. It is full of extraordinary things which are not always useful; often, they become distractions, if you want to live fully.'

'That is the whole point of living, isn't it?'

Now, thought-provoking silence engulfs the air. There is something about silence. Words cannot express its beauty; that would be like explaining the meaning of a word by remaining silent. The power of silence is something else. You sit still and observe it, without listening or uttering a word, without even any thoughts in your head. When you observe this silence, perfection begins to emerge in your being. It is a blissful experience. It can only be felt in silence and is difficult to explain in words.

The damp wood crackles as the fire takes centre stage. The fire surges up. We sit around it hypnotized with our legs criss-crossed and fold our hands, as we prepare for the prayer. The chanting begins. We raise and move our hands as the prayers continue. The feeling is extraordinary. One of the women plays the rattle drum. Our heads start moving by themselves. Our bodies sway to the music.

I stare at the fire, my gaze affixed at its glow. It's a part of us, the fire. We look deep into it, searching for familiar patterns or forms. The same usually happens when we stare at the other elements that make us. The sight immediately makes us feel alive. I cannot stop looking at it again. The fire rises and flows into the night sky. I follow its path, I merge with it. It's a feeling of oneness. The ecstasy is breathtaking, in the most literal sense. I take a deep breath and then breathe out. The chanting grows intense. May there be peace! May there be an end to suffering! We chant together. As I exhale, I find myself coming out of my body and moving towards the moonlit forest.

Is this really happening?

I look at the sky and it is full of stars. There are the seven stars, which look distinctly familiar. The full moon looks gigantic from here. I stare at it as I bathe in its glory. I look at my hand and wonder if the moon and I share the same stardust. It is as if I am the moon, and I am looking at the earth in the sky with seven of them sitting close to me. It feels surreal.

I look back at the fire from a distance. Everyone is sitting around it. The seven of them. They are twinkling like stars. There is something about the number seven. There are seven oceans, seven continents, seven wonders, seven days, seven colours of the rainbow, seven heavens even . . . It's a number of completeness and perfection. Wherever you go, this number comes up on its own. You do not have to think or learn about it; you just look at this number and you feel a connection with it. If you think about a number, it surfaces in your mind. Such is the beauty of the number seven. It's divine. I look at them and count them. Seven. Yes indeed, that's the number.

But wait . . . that looks . . . that looks like me. Am I looking at myself? I have left everything behind and come here. It has happened before, I recall. But unlike the previous time, I do not feel scared or worried. I feel blissful. It is quiet and serene here.

I continue exploring the woods. Initially, it seemed to be dark out here, but as I walk deeper, I observe there is light all around. Fireflies are twinkling through the leaf litter; it feels as though I am surrounded by hundreds of Christmas trees. The rocks are glowing and the trunks of the trees are sparkling too. It's as if there is a sky up there and there is a sky down here. It's a beautiful sight. I sit on the branch of a tree and watch the two worlds come in contact through my existence. I hear a sound. I turn to the other side to see what it is. I see myself sitting across the branch. I look closely at this figure who appears exactly like me. I move towards him. I try to tell him that I am not different. *Hoot! Hoot!* I say, or manage to say, as no other words come out. Who are you? Are we any different? Is it just me going around in circles and seeing the world through different eyes?

I spend what seems like a lifetime in that place, looking at myself.

The next moment, I open my eyes. Did I just blink or witness this bliss for what seemed like an eternity? I look around. I am sitting in the same place where I was earlier. Next to the fire. They are still singing and dancing. I am a part of them too, although a little confused. I cannot believe what just transpired. But, I know it happened. I continue to look into the fire and hear the chants that float in the air, and become one with the light and the sound.

In the morning when I wake up, it is another glorious day. I look around and there is no one to be seen. I am all alone, or am I? Where are those men and women? Perhaps they have gone back to where they came from. Perhaps it was all a dream. There is just me. It has always been me. I am the whole world. That is all there is. I think I have found the answer. It is here. In this place. It is what I was looking for. I get up and walk into the forest and keep walking until I reach the end of it.

What is this? I wonder.

I look at this place. The waterfall—isn't it . . . and . . . next to it, what is that which looks familiar? No way! Have I reached the cave?

Chapter 8

The Genius Within

A few moments glide by, as the wind whispers. I stand outside the cave and sense many thoughts popping inside my head—some questions seeking closure, some answers looking for their origins. I can hear myself huffing and puffing, my heart pumping. The music flows in our breath, sometimes gentle and sometimes rapid. Right now, it is more like the latter.

It was a long journey in terms of distance, albeit short in time. I did not realize how far I had travelled until I had arrived here and watched the tiredness take over. Now, I just want to lie down and rest. *Some sleep would be nice*, I tell my aching body. The thought takes me away from tiredness, into the realm of comfort. Here and now. It's a curious thing—the thought. It can shift your perspective in an instant.

As I am about to take a step in, I pause and turn around to have a look at the valley. It's a sight to behold! I am already short of breath, and it takes away whatever I am left with. The valley looks the same, and yet different. It is like a new day—the same sun illuminates the same earth in exactly the same way, but it feels different every time. I look at myself and there seem to be many changes. Is it the same me that came here last year? So many cells of my body have been replaced by new ones. However, I believe my true essence has been there, without any change or interruption. The self experiences and that is all it does—without judgement, without biases. It experiences the entire universe through a speck of the universe itself, my body, in which it resides.

I turn to the cave and, once again, as I am about to step in, I pause mid-air and . . . within a second, I bend backwards, almost as if I am dodging a bullet. Swoosh! A bird flies past me, grazing my cheek with its talons. 'You almost killed me,' I say, looking back at it. I turn to the cave again and . . . wait, what is that, inside? I inspect the cave inquisitively. There is noticeable movement. Could that be a leopard or a bear that scared that bird? I can't tell, but there is definitely something inside the cave. *I must tread carefully*, I think to myself and immediately get into alert mode. Gently, I take a step back. There is curiosity in my mind, still. What could it be? I peek through the corner of my eye—nothing to be seen.

I look at the entrance and then inside. There is light inside, much brighter than I would expect. 'Is that real?'

I whisper. A white glow hovers in the cave and moves quickly when I look at it. I want to look away, but I am mesmerized and I cannot. It pulls me towards itself and all my attention gravitates . . . and the moment I turn to it, I can no longer see it. Because as soon as I look at it, it hides and then reappears somewhere next to where I am looking now. I chase it and it keeps disappearing and reappearing. There is something at work here. Something otherworldly. Without thinking anything about the consequences of it, I walk inside.

The cave feels unusually warm today. I sense it the moment I take the first step, and it keeps getting warmer, as if the seasons are changing with each step. My skin is being engulfed by a layer of warmth around it. How is this even happening? It is cold outside—and there is no fire in here. What is it that surrounds me? I leave these questions aside when I see a figure right in front of my eyes. I try to focus on it. It's a man; he is sitting still, showing no concern about what is going on around him. There is no movement, no sound, nothing. The air is still, acknowledging the perfect silence that surrounds it. I can even hear the smallest of movements in my body. I stand still and look at the man again. *Who could that be?* I ask myself. Adi? No, he seems much shorter than Adi. Now, as I step forward, I get a glimpse of his face too. He is definitely not Adi, or anyone that I have seen before. But who is he? I stare at his face for the next few moments, wave after wave after wave, the questions rise and fall in my head. The more I stare, the stranger I feel about the whole situation. The calmness on his face is not disturbed by my presence.

'Hello,' I say and move closer to the man. 'Can we have a word please?'

No response. I lean forward, with my face next to his, and say again. 'Hello, sorry to disturb you, but . . . umm, is it all right if I stay here for a bit?' Still nothing. His eyes are closed. His hands rest on his thighs. His spine is perfectly straight and so is his neck. He seems to be in a blissful state, in a place far away from the chaos of our world. There is no movement in his body. It is as still as it can be. I tap his shoulder gently. Nothing this time either. I watch carefully and check his head and face. Wait a second . . . what? He is not breathing. How can that be? This is not possible. So, I place my hand on his chest. The heartbeat—there is none. I check again, just to be sure—and there is nothing. Then the pulse. No sign there, either. I clench it firmer, try as hard as I can. Is he really dead? No, he cannot be—his body is so warm.

I do not know what to make of this situation. I leave the cave for a few days and come back to find a dead man sitting in here. What in the god's name is going on? The question looms in front of me—what do I do now? I sit in the opposite corner and look at him. The calm on his face is such that I cannot look at him for long—nor can I look away. I feel a strange surge of activity between my eyebrows, somewhere deep within my skull when I look at him. It is a bittersweet sensation, and it seems oddly comforting.

I spend some time resting against the rock and weighing my options. I don't know how much time goes by, but it feels like a really, really long time. Surprisingly, the shadows in the cave have not moved an inch. Has the time stopped? I try to recollect everything in my head. Where have I reached? What was I doing on the previous evening? I cover my face with my hands and sigh. 'Can anyone please tell me what is going on here?' I ask.

There is a sound from the other side! A voice, resonating and baritone. Overpowered by shock and fear, I do not understand it. To my own surprise, I choose to hang on and not run away. Sometimes, all you have is your instinct and it's a blessing.

'Go back, this is not the place to be,' the voice echoes. 'Go back, go back, go back,' it keeps on repeating. I keep my eyes closed and listen, until the voice fades in the distance. It is mysterious, perhaps something extraordinary is at work here and I do not want to miss this opportunity to make sense of what resides outside our common sense experiences. So I choose to have faith and stay. I look up and everything is still the same. It can't be. Was it my mind telling me to go back? I have heard the stories of hallucinations when people encounter a situation of extreme fear. Could it be that? Perhaps . . .

I decide to befriend my fears and stay.

When the evening arrives, the cold wind comes piercing into the cave and I turn to the fire that I sparked a few minutes back. I get a strange comfort sitting next to the fire as the wind touches my body. *Soulful*, I tell myself. There is a sense of fatigue in my body, but the eerie feeling in my heart has been replaced by solace. I don't know whether I am falling asleep or visualizing something—it's surreal. 'This feels so good,'

I say. A moment later, I open my eyes when I hear a voice saying, 'That's not too bad.'

As I raise my head, I turn my gaze to the man and, to my surprise, he is sitting there with eyes wide open. What? I see his smiling, beady eyes. I get scared for a moment and crawl back. Now, my back is against the proverbial wall and I am unable to go any further. 'What is going on?' I ask in a low voice. 'Could you please tell me?'

'Don't worry. It is all right,' he says once again, with a smile on his face. That does not comfort me one bit. But since, here inside this cave, away from the rest of the world, my choices are limited, I choose to believe him.

'Are you all right?' he inquires.

'I don't know. I just came back to the cave, and when I saw you, I thought you were not well. You seemed . . . how do I say it? Dead! That is what caused me to react this way. I am sorry about that.'

I keep rambling.

'You do not need to fear, it is not good for you,' he says. 'Take a deep breath. You have made a long journey.' I understand his words, but right now, it does not seem to make any difference. Fear operates in its own ways. It grabs you by your jaws and does not release you, no matter how much you wish it to. I feel overpowered and helpless.

'But how is it possible?' I ask, hoping to find my answers. 'You were not breathing. I checked it myself. I checked your heartbeat, your pulse. You were not alive. It cannot be a dream. I saw it, experienced it. It was real.'

'Well,' he says, 'if you go back and tell anybody that, they are not going to believe you. Nobody believes these kinds of things these days. So, there is no point in repeating it. People might think that you are out of your mind.'

'But you know it,' I protest. 'You know that I have not lost my marbles. That this is the truth. There is something that you know and I don't.'

'Of course, I know that,' he says and closes his eyes briefly. 'Do you really think I am unaware of what you just witnessed?'

'Tell me,' I say in exasperation. 'Tell me, how is it possible? How did you do that?'

'I am sorry,' he responds, looking into my eyes, 'but I cannot reveal that. I cannot share this with anyone without the consent of my master. He is the one who showed me the path.'

I don't know what to say. So, I take a moment to recollect my thoughts. As I breathe deeply, the thoughts arrange themselves coherently and transform into speech.

'I don't understand,' I say. 'Isn't it good to share your wisdom?'

'It is,' he says, calmly. 'But, you know, sometimes we can also help others by keeping our secrets to ourselves. Only those who are capable of embarking on this long journey can grasp these mysteries. This path—it's not for everyone. There are far too many distractions. When one takes this path, he gets obsessed with the very first things he sees and gets absorbed in their amusements. It is not healthy, it limits his growth.

So, it should not surprise us that we hardly get to meet any enlightened souls. They usually live away from crowds. No one really knows their whereabouts, but they do what they have to.'

'I understand. I won't ask your secret. What would I do with it anyway?' I say. The conversation is starting to ease my concerns. So, I decide to continue. 'Tell me, is it possible for a man to develop control over his heartbeat?'

'You are not going to let this go, are you?' he laughs. 'Let me explain. It is the control over one's body. Most people, most of the time, do not have much control over their body or mind. They give in to impulses. But some develop this control. How much control one can develop, to what extent—that is another matter altogether.'

'What do you mean?' I ask.

'I mean, the extent to which you control your body. You can do that with your breathing. How much you can expand it, manage it, hold it—that can have consequences that everyone cannot fathom.'

'It's how we spend the limited amount of air we have been blessed with, isn't it? Dogs breathe rapidly and have shorter life spans compared to a tortoise that breathes about four times every minute. Breath is what gives us life—it is the second layer of existence inside this physical sheath.'

'You seem to know quite a bit,' he says and I get his endorsement. He scrutinizes me from head to toe. 'One can find whatever one is seeking. The point is, this is one aspect of developing control over your body. With practice, you can get more specific as you dive deeper. That way you can develop control over every organ and even the body itself. The blood flow, the heartbeats, the brain activity—all these can be controlled only through intense practice.'

'In the same way, one needs to work on the mind as well?'

'Most definitely,' he says. 'Mastering the mind is even more important than mastering the body. It is only through your mind that you are going to exert your will on the body. If the mind is not under your control, then it will keep deceiving you and make you do all kinds of impulsive things, which will keep you away from the ultimate reality. Life becomes an endless cycle of pleasure and pain, and by the time you want to reflect, death is knocking at the door. This is what happens with most people. Thankfully, some try to get over this barrier. Once you are on the path, you can do things which would seem irrational to a rational mind.'

'Yes, I understand what you mean,' I say, and take a moment to reflect. 'Can't you tell me anything about your master? Or is that a secret too?'

'Well . . .' he hesitates, but goes on. 'He is an open book, but written in an indecipherable text. He is here, and he is not. He teaches things that one already knows, but has forgotten. You will find him only when the time is right.'

'He sounds like an enigma. Can I ask something about you, please? All this mystery is getting to be too much for me.'

'What about me?' he asks, almost laughingly. 'I am right here in front of you. In this moment, your awareness knows more about me than it knows about anything else in the world.'

'No, I mean . . . about you. How long have you been here? How did you get here?'

'I can tell you that surely,' he says smiling, 'but I don't think you will believe me.'

'I will believe you,' I say with conviction. 'What is there not to believe?'

'All right,' he says. 'Let me tell you then. I was meditating for a few moments.'

'That can't be . . .' I say.

'You promised to believe me,' he says, laughing. 'Time works differently for everyone—you just told me about dogs and tortoises, remember?'

I smile.

He continues, 'I have been staying here for many years. Not just seasons, hundreds of seasons. I have spent every single day of these seasons in this cave, only venturing out when I needed to fill my rumbling belly or charge my batteries.'

'But . . . I was here,' I hesitate. 'I was right here, in this cave. For the last one year, I have been here. I know this place far too well. I never saw you. How is—'

'Just breathe,' he says. 'You don't have to understand, but experience.'

His words sound oddly familiar. Haven't I had this conversation before?

'These mountains are full of such caves. Sometimes, you cannot tell which one is which. Also, some of these caves are not static. They move, from here to there. They alter shapes. They talk, if you listen to them. They welcome you, as if you are not lost but have returned home. People are all too busy to listen to these things. They think that they are the masters of this world and the world is their slave. So, they don't possess any sensitivity to understand things that don't talk or walk like them. Things are just dead, people claim, and move on to more interesting things in their lives. But, if you are willing to open your eyes and ears—and I can see that you are—you will not only witness magic in every moment but live it as well.'

I look around when he says these words. Every corner, every stone in the cave is so similar. I cannot believe that it is any other cave than the one that I had left behind. Or, hang on, is it? There is a difference, I suspect, and it begins to emerge as soon as the doubts creep into my mind. When I look at those figures on the carvings, they seem no less real than reality. They seem to move and speak, all at once. I rub my eyes and press my ears—still, no respite. Suddenly, there seems to be a flood of sound and light—it all flies towards me and I have to close my eyes and ears. I scream in anguish.

'It's all right,' the man says in a loud voice and the surroundings begin to calm. 'Since you have decided to embrace these new experiences, I want you to know that you are safe here.' I hear only his voice and the rest of the chatter dies down. 'Now do you understand why all of this is a secret? One may find such experiences troubling. One may not be able to make sense of reality. The reality that is kept hidden to us by our physical boundaries.'

'How do you live here?' I ask, thinking of what he just said. 'Do you keep any stuff here?'

'What stuff? There is no stuff. There is just one thing and that thing is me,' he says. Isn't the same conversation repeating itself? Except this time, I am Dev.

My question might have been out of restlessness, but his answer is not. 'This might be unbearable for most people, as it might be unbearable for me to live like they do. For me, there is a whole world here in the mountains, in the cave, in myself. It is far too interesting to miss out on. When you are at ease with yourself, life seems comfortable. And this is my comfort. Rarely does anyone come here, and when they do, they cannot make sense of it, whether I am alive or not. So, they leave.'

'I see,' I nod. 'You know, I have stayed here for a year, and food has been difficult to come by. How have you managed that? I don't see much to eat around here.'

'You don't need much when your goal is survival. Only this much will do,' he makes a gesture with his hand, suggesting that a handful is enough. 'I eat once, or twice, a week. When the winters arrive, even less than that. Yes, water, I drink in plenty. Thankfully, there is no shortage of water here.'

'Really?' I ask. 'Is it possible to survive with that kind of diet? I would think that after some time, you would feel the need to eat something more.'

'That is also because,' he says, looking at me, 'of how one controls his body and mind, lest they start controlling him. This body is a system, a machine. The most remarkable machine in the world, if you ask me. So precisely designed, so delicately balanced. It does not need as much fuel as we often put into it, nor does it need the fuel in the same form. What it needs is,' he pauses and stretches his arms wide apart, 'energy. The balance of energy, rather. If one can create that balance inside, so that a small amount of energy is required to sustain this system, then one can bring both longevity and efficiency to this system. Besides, how you spend your energy—that also matters. The balance inside and outside—both are important. That way, you can absorb the energy from outside and create a balance inside. And once you achieve this, life goes on, the way it is supposed to.'

'I am not sure how to ask this, but how old are you?'

He laughs and laughs; it goes on for a while. 'No problem,' he says. 'It is a perfectly reasonable question. I have lost count. I have witnessed hundreds and hundreds of seasons change.'

'What!' I say, as I cannot control my raised eyebrow. 'You look extremely fit,' I say, while scrutinizing his lean body. Even his skin seems youthful.

'Well, you can do that. I remember a phrase from my time in the city. That age is just a number. I would say, age is just a way to tell how one looks after himself. It is entirely up to us to decide how to lead our life, what to do with our body and mind. If you look after them, they don't get affected very much. It is like having a car.

How you keep it, how well you drive it, how you use it, or overuse it. We always have that choice with our bodies too. Yet, we rarely exercise that choice. The pleasures of the world are too many, and often too enjoyable, to overcome and get to the other side.'

'Why did you leave it then? The city, I mean,' I ask. It feels as though I am talking to myself from the past or the future. No, it cannot be. I pinch myself and focus on what is unfolding before me.

'It's a long story,' he says. 'I have tried living in different places, exploring different ways to find answers. It has been a long time since I realized that city life was not for me. Such tightly knit societies without much of a connection. It was then I realized an important life lesson. That it was better to be alone than to walk with a fool. The fool might take you in the wrong direction, and the journey might become meaningless. Societal systems never made sense to me. Clearly, I was not fond of them and that is why I am here. It came to a stage where it bothered me—the noises, the chaos, the greed, the lack of compassion, the abundance of fear. It was suffocating. People competing with one another as if they took the idea of the human race literally. There, we were thinking more from our heads and less from our hearts and acting compulsively. That thought crept into my head too. That I too would end up becoming compulsive and lose my way. So, I asked myself—freedom or city life? I chose the life of a caveman.'

'You know, I have had the exact same thoughts when I was trying to meditate in the cave. I cannot believe this. Every word of it—I have felt them exactly in the same way.'

'Is that so?' he asks, looking deep into my eyes.

'Yes,' I say, trying hard to focus. 'However, there was a difference. I thought, surely it was better to walk alone than walk with a fool, but I kept hoping that it would be better to walk with the wise than walk alone.'

'That is strange indeed, as I have wondered about this in all these years. That, what would have happened had I taken the other path?'

'Well, here I am, your answer. But you knew that, didn't you?'

We look at each other for a while. I think about a lot of things, but above all, I think about what he is thinking—perhaps he is thinking the same. It's a rare moment, that of one seeing oneself, without turning inwards.

'I did,' he says, bowing his head gently.

As he bows his head, I get a glimpse of a passage behind. 'What is that?' I ask.

'You can see that?' he says. 'It's time then, you are ready.'

He gets up and walks towards the passage. I follow him.

As we stare into it, there are not one but many passages—each leading to others. On the rocks surrounding the passage, there are several figures carved in circles. Some look familiar, like the people and the places I have seen before, and some are completely unknown. However, on closer inspection, it reveals an unexpected picture: there is a hand carved in the centre, then there is the sun and the planets around it, forming the solar system; the solar system then leads to the galaxy which leads to the infinite cosmos. I place my hand on the carving and it fits perfectly. The next moment, I am somewhere else.

I am the air, blowing on a mountaintop. I am the river uniting with the ocean. I am here and I am there too. It seems as though I am the ever-expanding universe. It is similar to an infinitely complex spider web where every thread is interconnected and I am present in every one of them. Where is the spider, though?

The moment this question arises, I find myself in the same spot where I was earlier, looking at the carvings. It feels as if someone has woken me up from a dream. I see a hand on my shoulder. Am I awake?

We look into the passage again.

'Have you explored some of these?' I ask.

'Many, I should say. This one, on the right, will take you to places of great inspiration. A mountain with a sacred symbol. A river with holy origins. An ocean with divine connections. Some go to the past, some to the future and some to the subterranean world.'

'You are not taking me for a fool, are you?'

'Why don't you see for yourself?'

I take a step forward and walk into the passage. 'What is hap—'

Everything fades—the sound, the light, the world around. Everything. My hands, my legs, all my body—they are gone too. Nothing moves, only stillness remains; no sounds, no troubles, only silence and tranquillity prevail. All the doubts, all the fears dissolve in this calm. There is existence—that's all. It takes different forms, grows and decays, but it goes on.

I am the spider, I realize. And I am the web. I am the cause as well as the effect. I see it now.

Once again, I wake up from this dream. I feel I have been here before. This is a powerful déjà vu moment. This happened when I made the inward journey in the cave. Didn't I enter one such passage, then?

We look at each other again. The answers have revealed themselves to me.

'I hope you are at peace now,' he says with a smile. 'What you are following is your path, what I am following is mine.'

'It is the only thing that separates us—the path.'

'That's right. The path that we choose to walk on defines who we are. When the path ends, the journey continues, on a different path.'

'What do you mean?'

'The paths that we lay down through our wills. Every moment, we have a choice. The choice we make, it naturally opens a new door and takes us to a new world. The paths are many and so are the worlds. One makes a choice and creates his own. The diversity of life around us, the expansion of the universe—it's not a coincidence, or is it? Think of all the people you have met on your journey. Were they not the manifestations of your deepest desires and fears?'

I think and remember all the faces on my journey. I wanted to be the guy who would run away from college and travel. I was also the one who tried to understand consciousness. I feared losing my loved ones. I thought about leaving everything behind and praying in the sacred mountains. All that came true and for that I am grateful. It's just that I saw it from a narrow perspective and thought that they were they and I was I. However, there was no such distinction.

'What do I do from here?' I ask.

'What does your heart say? That is all that matters. You don't have to tell me. Just put your hand on your heart and listen to it.'

'Let me do that.' I close my eyes and put my hand on my heart. The two immediately connect and speak to each other. Strangely, I am merely an observer in this conversation.

'I think . . .' I say after some time. 'I have not left the world behind me. I want to be with it, participate in it, play in it. It is not an addiction. I could live here happily. But, I also see the meaning in the service of others.'

'Then, that is what you should do,' he says and blesses me.

'You know,' I say, 'I also recognize the transient nature of the physical body, the world around me and the universe itself. I have come to realize that even when I am with people, I need to find time for myself. So that the journey inwards goes on. It does not have to stop because of others. Their presence can make it better too, if I am willing to learn in challenging circumstances.'

'If you recognize the ultimate truth, that is it. This realization itself is enough. Now, whether you walk slowly or at a quick pace, you will get there. I came to live in the mountains not because all the answers are here, but because it was best suited for me to find the answers. Similarly, there will be different places suitable for different beings. That is how you must make your choices. What you need is, the awareness. You live in the body, but you are not it. You live in the mind, but you are not it. Once that awareness is there, you will not get caught in the traps of the world. You will not suffer, but will help the world in dealing with its own suffering.'

'That is exactly what I wish to do. To help people in every capacity. To reduce their suffering. To make them happy.'

'Then, that is the path you must follow. There is only one person you need to be honest with, and that is you. Knowing yourself is the key to every lock. Since you know with all your heart and soul that your world is out there, then you should go there. Just go, then. Do not look back. Do not stop. The world is waiting for you.'

'Thank you,' I say.

'All right, then. Now, go and follow that path. Somewhere along the road, our paths shall cross once again. They always do. This is what my master has taught me.'

'Please give my regards to your master.'

'I will, and you can do that too. When you walk outside, you would see the footmarks on the snow. Really big ones. That will be him.'

'Thank you,' I stand up, and immediately it brings a smile to my face. 'I think I have found my answers. The ones which remain, I will find them too.' The wind comes from behind and blows out the fire. But it is not dark any more. The sunrays have found their way in. It's morning.

As I turn around, I get a sense that there is no one else in the cave. I want to look back, but I do not. Some things are not meant to be captured by the rational mind, or untangled. In the heart of our heart, we already know them. I smile once again. Nothing worries me.

I walk outside and turn around to have a look at the cave, for one last time. Then I glance at the waterfall and the landscape around. It seems like yesterday when I came here. But then, on second thought, I am not even sure if it was the same cave or the same me that came here. What I know is that the place has imprinted its memory on me. Everything flashes in my memory. All the things I witnessed here. All the people I met. The experiences I had. My family, back in the city. Then, I think of Adi.

I wonder where he is. I know where he is. He is around, always around, and never away. He guides me, shows me the path. As long as I have faith, I will keep finding him . . . and I do have that, now. I know that he is with me.

I turn towards the sky. The clouds have covered almost all of it. There it is. A snowflake. Gently, it falls on my face and melts immediately. I keep walking, the snow keeps falling. I look at the ground and see the big footmarks on it. The snow falls on them too. I deliberately walk, following the trail, towards human civilization. He is here, I am aware of it. I know in my heart, it's not the end. It's just the beginning.

Acknowledgements

I had been planning on putting this book together for a few years. I finally managed to piece this together and I couldn't have done it all by myself.

Firstly, I would like to thank Deepak Rana who contributed with research, structure and guidance to help put this book together. He worked tirelessly and kept challenging me to make the content more relevant for the readers.

My wife, Megha, for listening patiently through the hundreds of ideas I kept coming at her with and providing me valuable feedback. My mother Rita and my son Gautam also provided me with some brilliant inputs.

My friend Amber Amberkar and amazing colleagues and artists Aayush Kambli and Kajal Menghani for the artwork and design.

I am also very grateful to Brig. Kripalu, Col Nirbhai Marwaha and Sooman Marwaha, Anand Kripalu and Sukanya Kripalu, Vinod Kripalu and Chetana Kripalu,

Vinayak Sapru and Divya Ganesan, Naveen Panday and Deepika Panday, Sorabh Agrawal, Amit Chaudhary and Richa Chaudhary, Bin Srinidhi and Devi, Ujjwal Bhandari for their unwavering support. You were all there when I needed you.

And finally, to you, the reader, who has taken out the time to read this book.

I am grateful to all of you and I am humbled by your support.